# ABANDONED SOUTH TEXAS

## SHADOWS OF THE FORGOTTEN

TERESA NORDHEIM

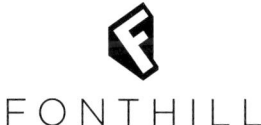

*To every warrior whose life has been altered by cancer and those who surrounded them with love and unconditional support.*

Fonthill Media Inc.
www.fonthillmedia.com
office@fonthillmedia.com

First published 2024

Copyright © Teresa Nordheim 2024

ISBN 978-1-62545-121-7

All rights reserved. No part of this publication may be reproduced, stored in a retrieval system or transmitted in any form or by any means, electronic, mechanical, photocopying, recording or otherwise, without prior permission in writing from Fonthill Media Inc.

Typeset in Trade Gothic 10pt on 15pt
Printed and bound in England

# CONTENTS

Acknowledgments  **5**

Introduction  **7**

1  Home Sweet Haunted Home  **17**

2  Boos Behind Bars  **34**

3  Paging Dr. Casper  **53**

4  Deserted Destinations  **72**

# ACKNOWLEDGMENTS

As 2022 ended, I found myself exhausted and depleted. The entire year vanished as I experienced countless treatments and surgeries to rid my body of cancer. This meant delaying my book and not enjoying my greatest comfort: writing. So, first and foremost, I want to thank God for granting me life, strength, and guiding the hands of my surgeons.

I also want to thank my publisher for their support and patience during this process. Despite the delays, they always placed my health above the due date.

I want to thank my family and friends who are always my biggest cheerleaders and give up the most during the writing process. Cindi and Katerina, you are always my strength and my greatest blessings. Nothing, especially this past year and this book, would be possible without your consistent love and support. Tyrani and Kim, your friendships are what keep me sane and make me laugh on the dark days. My work family, thank you for your continued support and for allowing me to tell ghost stories about our building.

Thank you to the photographers who helped add depth to the stories featured. Without your artistic abilities, this project would not be complete.

Lastly, God bless Texas and all the ghosts who refuse to leave.

# INTRODUCTION

South Texas, for this book, is the area south of Interstate 20 and includes many of the larger cities in the state. Some towns and locations sit abandoned and host a menagerie of ghosts.

First, it is essential to note that not all haunted places are void of people, and not all abandoned sites attract paranormal activity.

Abandonment occurs for many reasons, impacting a building or structure's history and present state. Ninety percent of the time, it all comes down to money. If a business fails to create a substantial income to outweigh its debt, the owner may close the company, or a bank may repossess the structure. The repair costs vary depending on the length of abandonment or the structure's condition. Many times, the cost of repair exceeds the building's value.

Another example is a building damaged by a natural disaster, such as a hurricane. The damage is too extreme to keep the facility open, but the repair or destruction cost exceeds the value. It often is free to leave a building in as-is condition, but demolition and repair always cost.

So, what happens to abandoned sites?

Some of these buildings will be destroyed and replaced by new structures. This route is often the most expensive and only used when necessary. Another option is to recycle or repurpose the building. While an old, historic, luxury hotel may require thousands of dollars to repair its former state, repurposed buildings become low-income housing or apartments for minimal cost. Repurposing is quite popular in urban developments as the historic architecture appeals to potential renters. Perhaps the most common outcome for an abandoned location is locking the doors and walking away. In the early years of abandonment, the structure remains frozen in time.

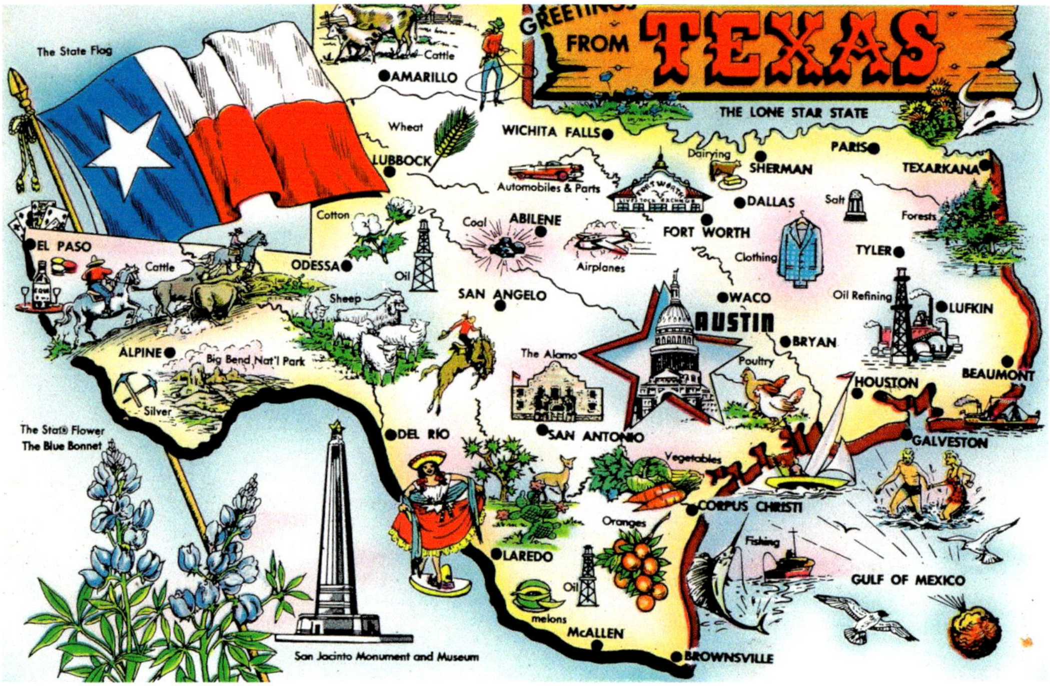

Postcard mapping the major cities in Texas. (*Author's collection*)

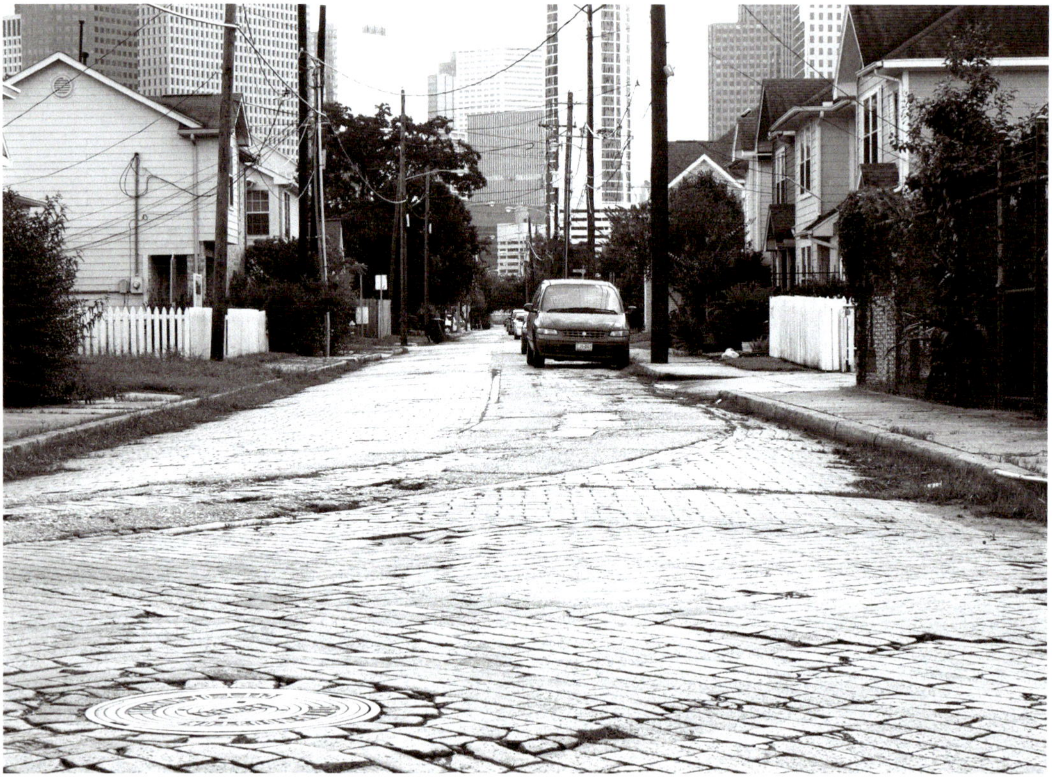

A view down an isolated street in Houston, Texas. (*Patrick Feller*)

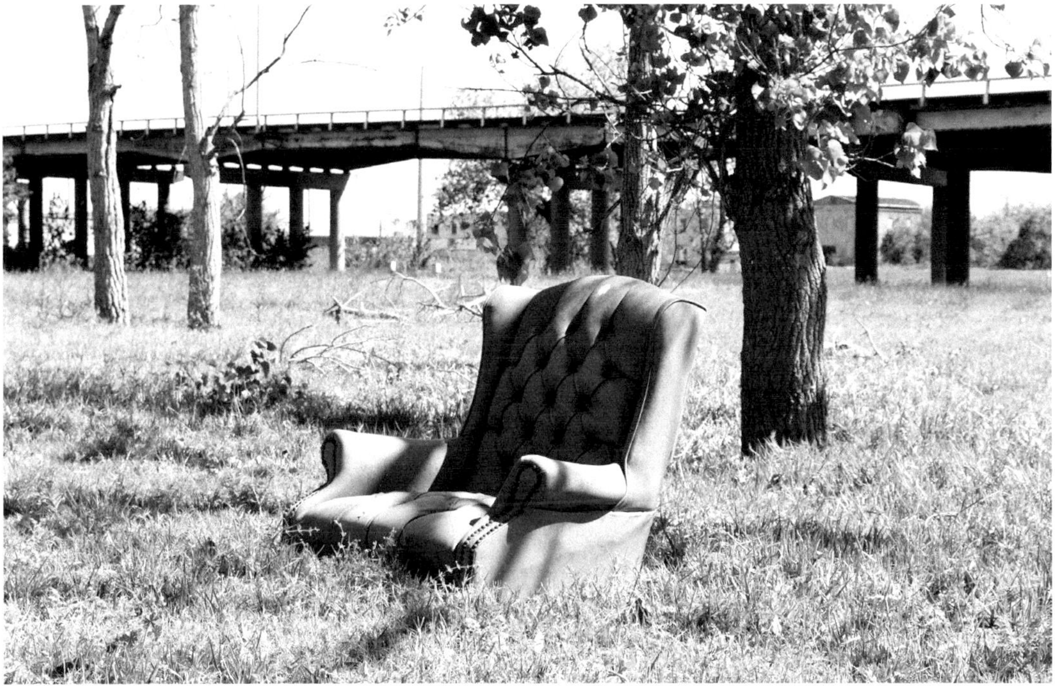

An abandoned and forgotten chair sits in the middle of a field. (*Patrick Feller*)

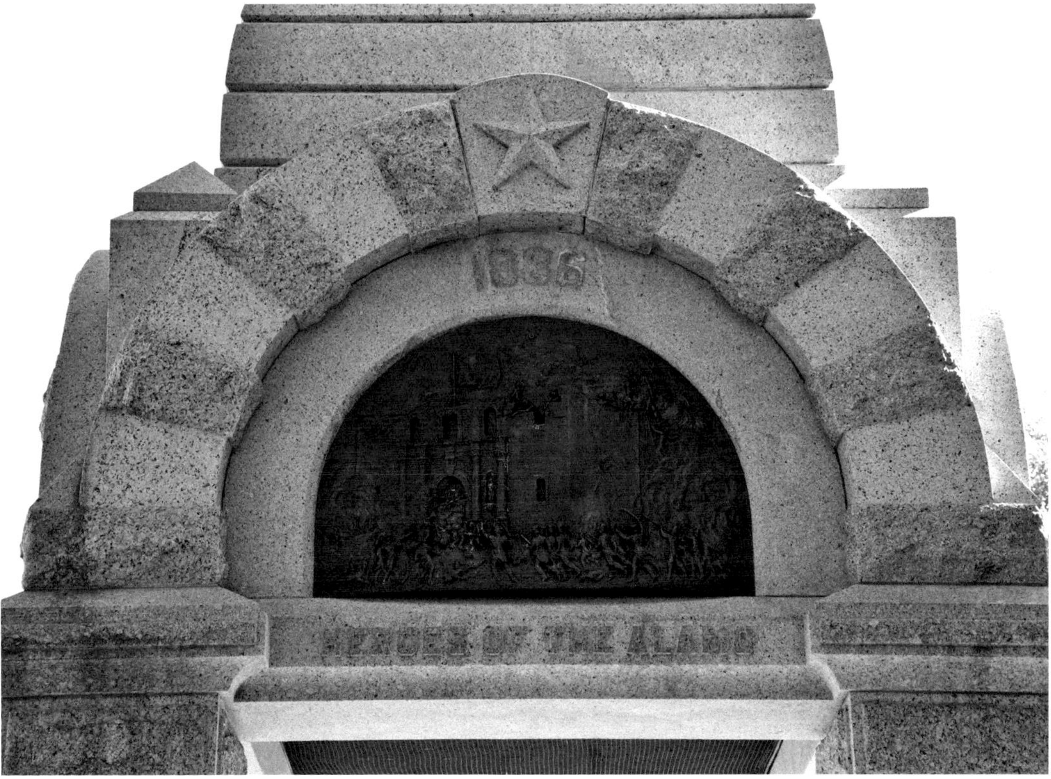

The historic Alamo was abandoned many years ago but is a tourist attraction today. (*Ken Lund*)

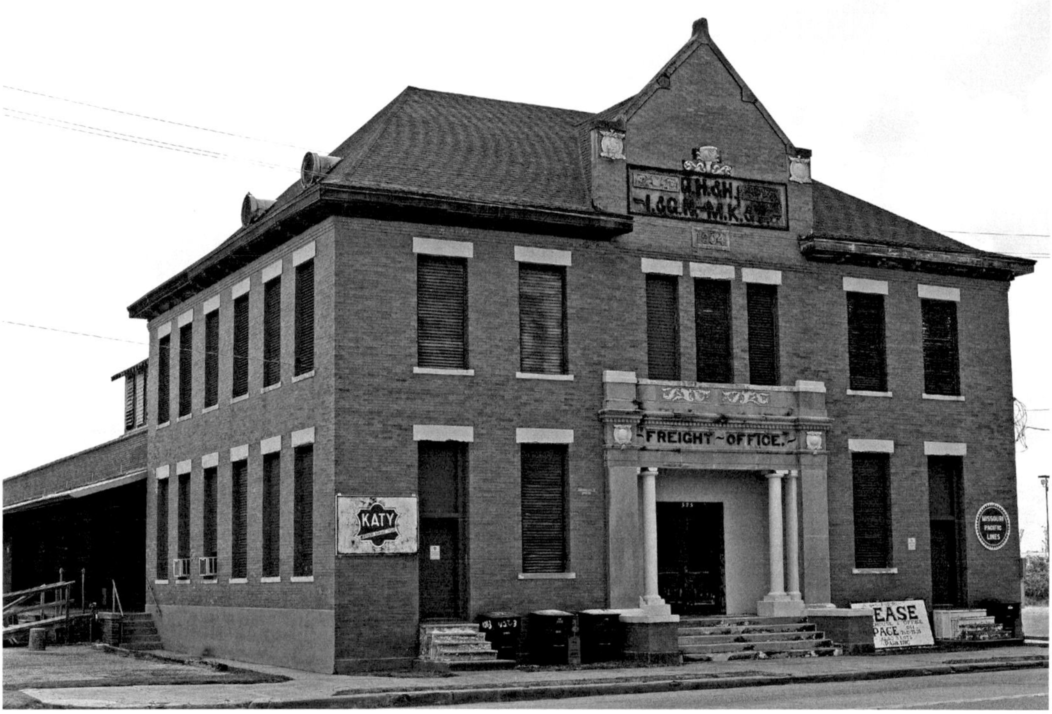

Sometimes abandoned buildings are graffitied by local gangs, rowdy teens, or troublemakers. (*Rob Sneed*)

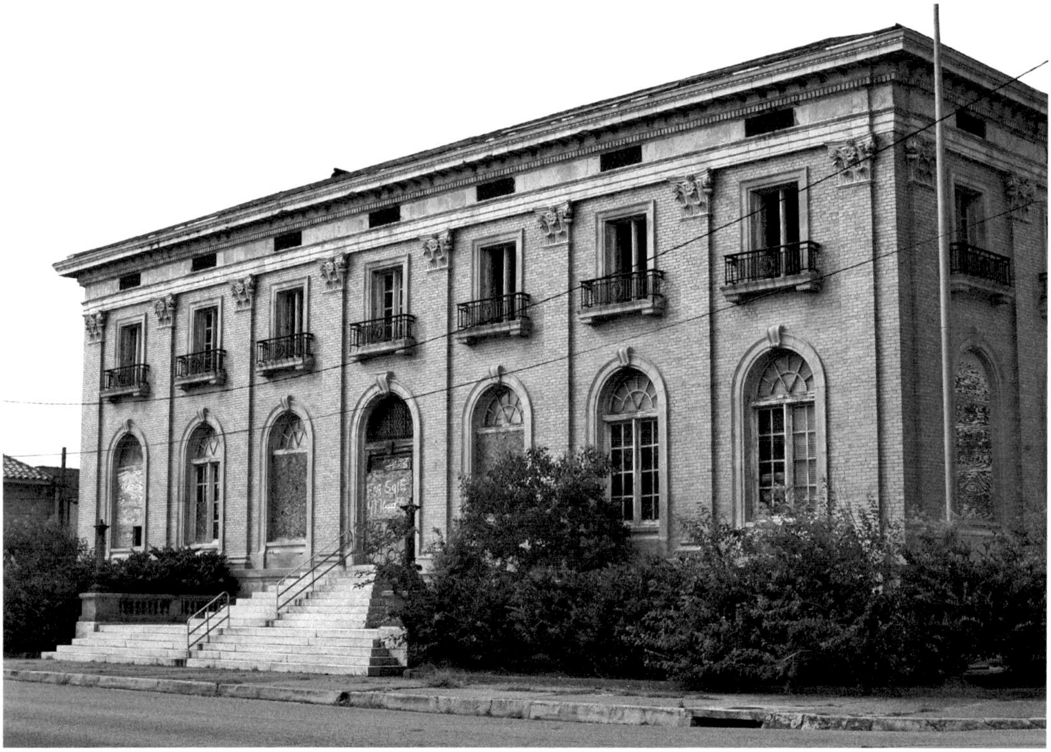

Abandoned hospitals and hotels are often refurbished as low-income apartment complexes. (*Rob Sneed*)

Urban explorers find these sites fascinating as they often offer a window to the past. The previous occupants might leave behind hints of the building's former identity. Historical papers, personal mementos, industrial equipment, and valuables remain in their original spots. A handful of people discover treasures awaiting them in abandoned structures. However, one of the first rules of urban exploration is to take nothing and only leave footprints. Respecting the area helps preserve the site for future explorers and is a sign of respect.

Exploration is not without risk. Exploring abandoned locations without permission could lead to arrest and jail. It is also important to understand that these sites are often in poor condition when vacated, significantly if natural disasters or vandals damage them. As time passes, wood rots, paint starts to peel, iron rusts, and even stones crumble. Safety is a considerable risk. Imagine falling through the wooden floor of a historic building, alone in the dark, unable to phone for help. A broken bone is far scarier than any paranormal encounter.

If the building sits undisturbed for an extended period, nature will begin reclaiming the land. Trees and plants sprout through the floors and walls.

The appearance of an abandoned location can appear haunting, but it does not mean ghosts linger in the halls. The question remains: do spirits move in when the living move out?

Many questions remain about the validity of apparitions. Advanced technology assists paranormal investigators, but it is crucial to remember that ghost hunting is not an exact science. Investigators utilize equipment to determine esoteric features in an environment.

Thermal cameras help determine changes in atmospheric temperature. Investigators will rule out air leaks from poorly sealed doors and windows if an area shows a cold spot. A small area of cold could be evidence of a ghostly presence.

Video and still cameras come in handy to snap pictures. Ghosts are not always visible to the human eye but can appear on video or photos. Investigators can snap random images and examine them as part of their research. It is handy to use a video recording device when attempting to speak to a ghost or aimed at a particular object which might draw the spirits, such as a personal item that belonged to the person while they were alive.

An EMF (electromagnetic field detection device) is one of the most common tools in every investigator's pocket. These devices detect changes in electromagnetic energy. They are not foolproof, but ghosts require energy to manifest. Therefore, a spike on the EMF meter can indicate a spirit attempting to communicate. However, industrial equipment and faulty wiring can also create elevations and interference on these meters.

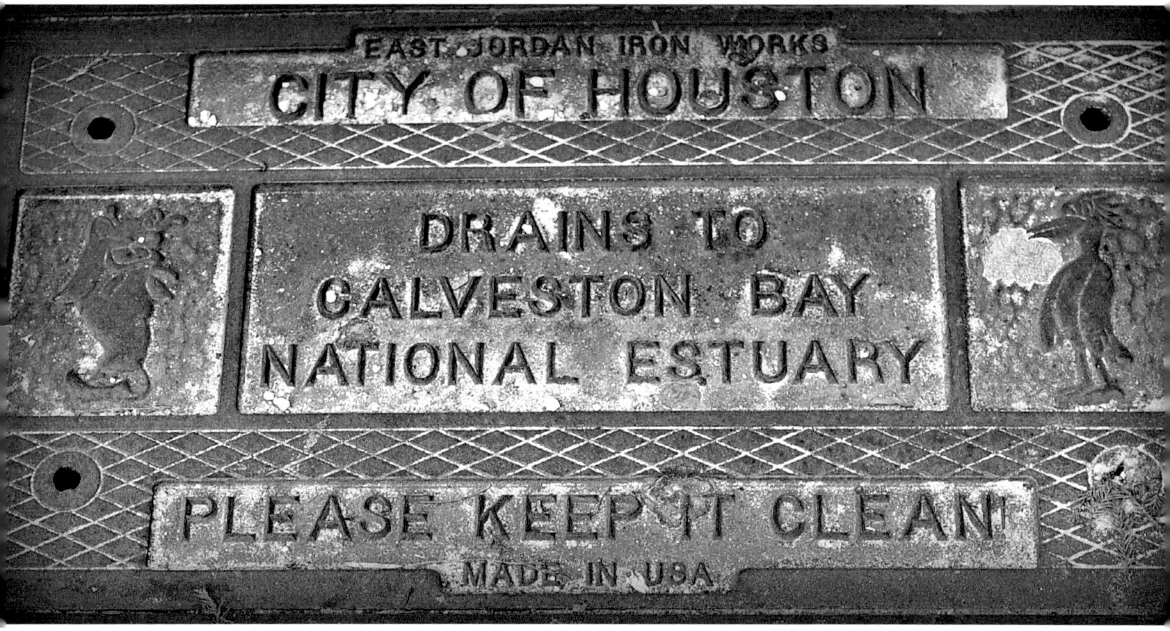

The grates in Houston appear rustic and fun. (*Rob Sneed*)

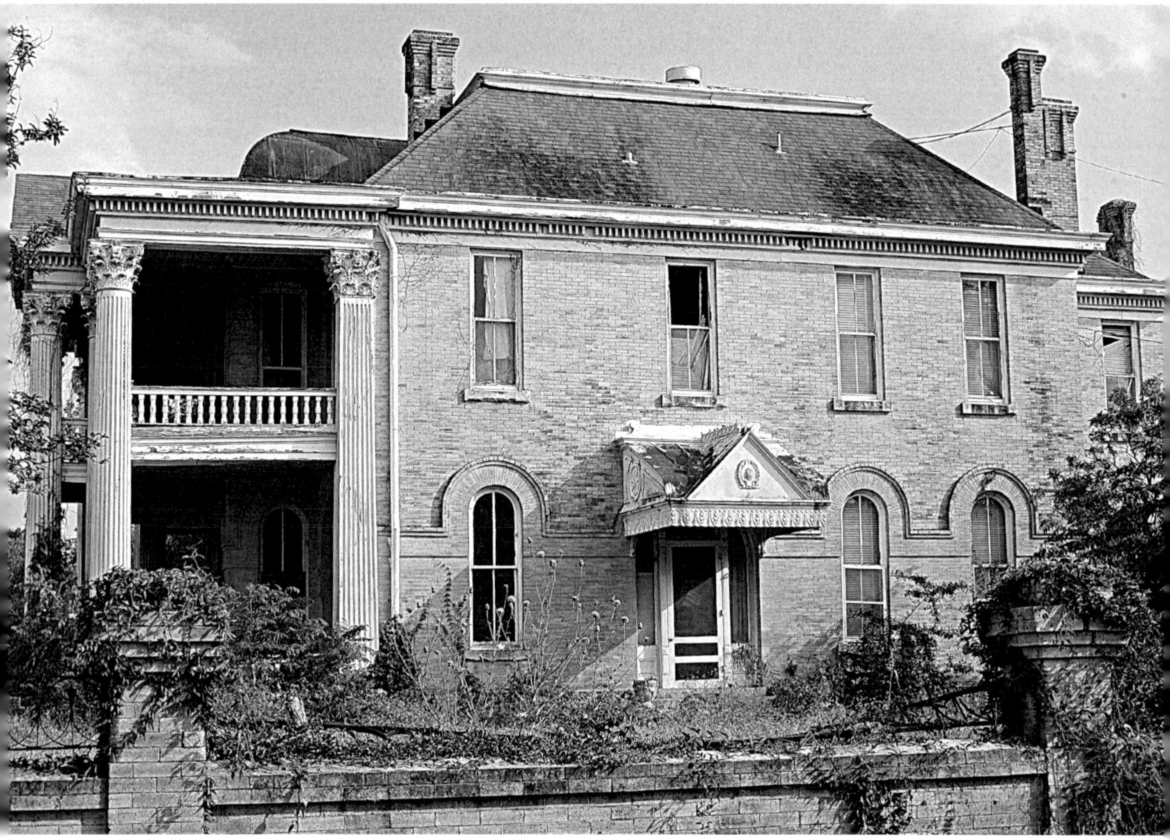

Walnut Ridge is a historic mansion challenged by the rough years of Texas weather. (*Rob Sneed*)

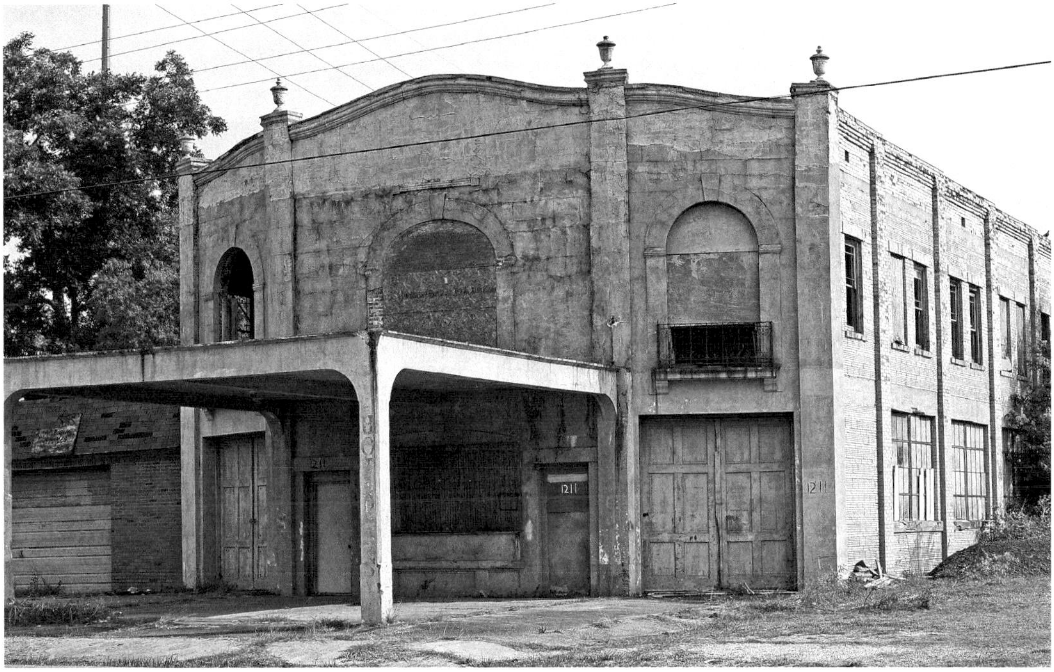

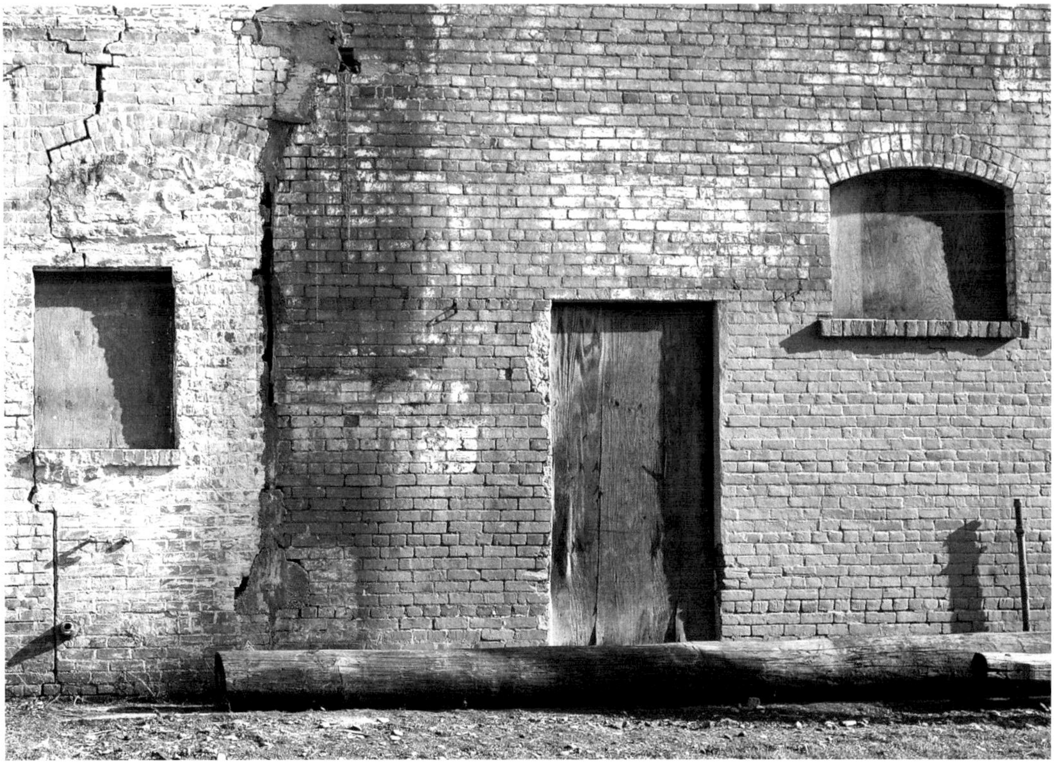

The owners of abandoned buildings often use wood or concrete to keep unwanted visitors outside the home. (*Rob Sneed*)

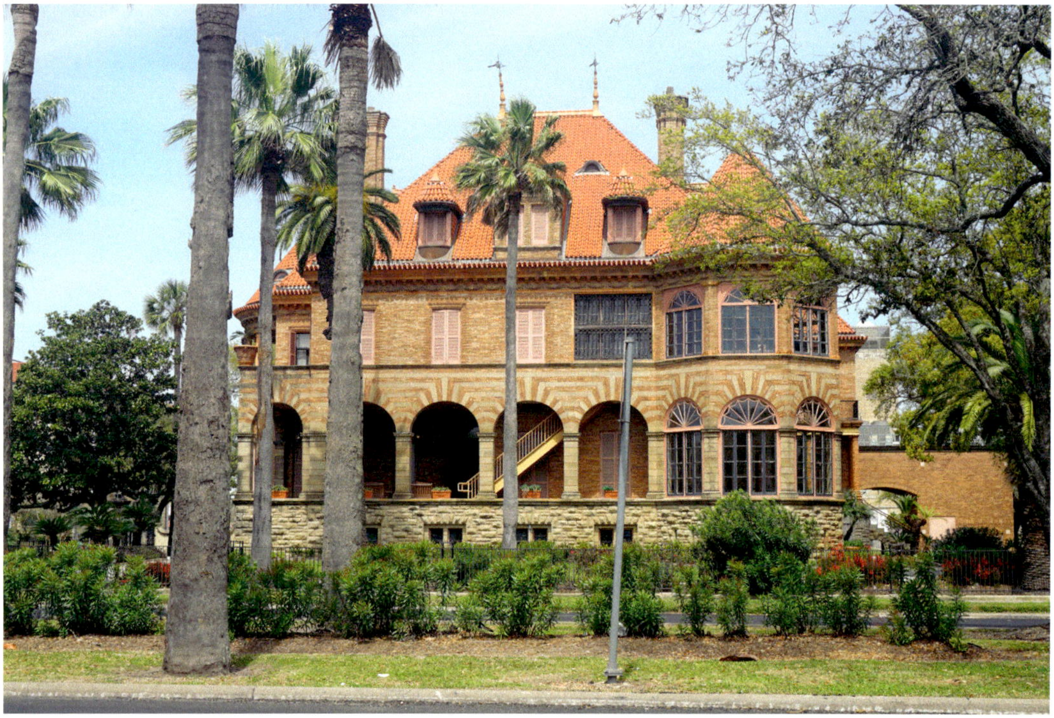

The Stewart mansion is a well-known abandoned mansion in Galveston, TX. (*Michael Barera*)

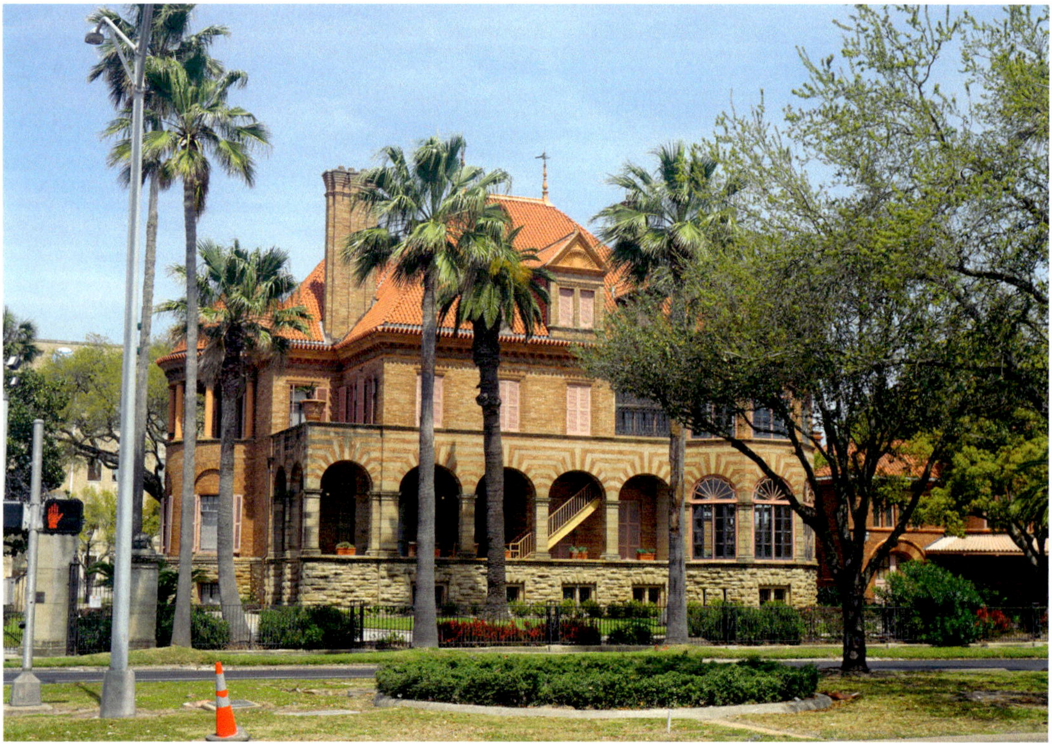

Another vital piece of equipment is a recording device. Using a small recording device to communicate with potential ghosts and gather noises undetectable via the human ears is essential. The discovery of an EVP (electronic voice phenomenon) is one of the most significant developments in paranormal research. Unexplainable noises and answers to investigative questions leave even the biggest skeptics pondering the possibilities of a ghostly encounter.

Welcome to South Texas's abandoned, haunted, and beautiful sites.

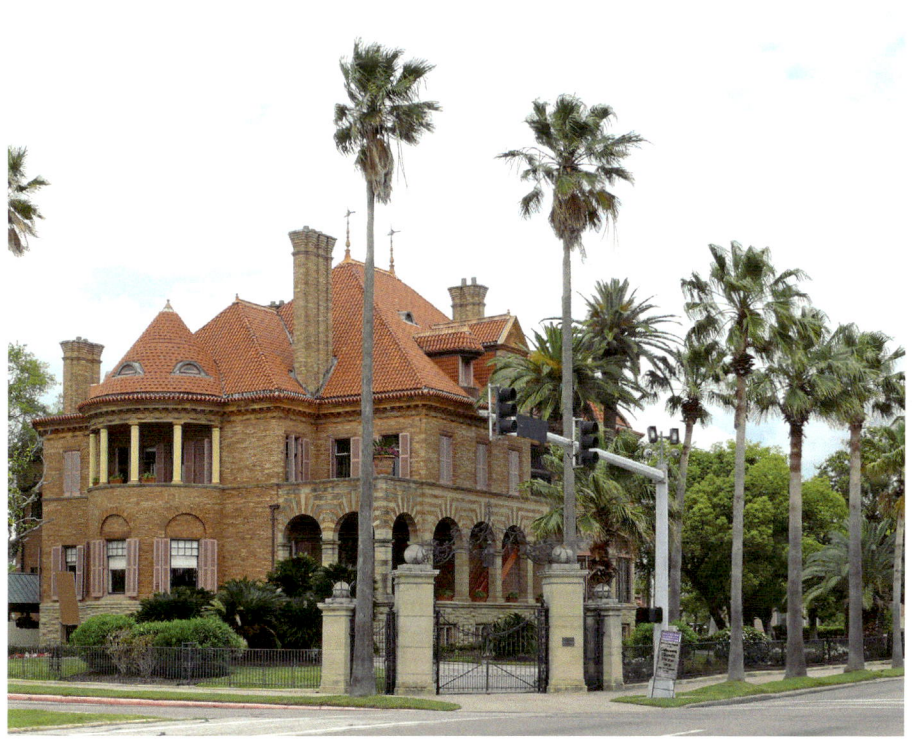

The turrets offer a Victorian feel to the mansion. (*Michael Barera*)

# 1

# HOME SWEET HAUNTED HOME

## Stewart Mansion

George Sealy II was a businessman born in Galveston, Texas, on December 13, 1880. Sealy was the eldest of eight children born to a wealthy businessman named George Sealy and his wife, Magnolia. Sealy lived a luxurious life and received business training from his father and cousin. When his father passed in 1901, Sealy quickly put his training and degree to work to care for his siblings and aging mother. He graduated from Princeton University in 1902.

At forty-three, Sealy married late in life to a beautiful young woman named Eugena Taylor. She was only twenty-two then, but the couple remained married and had three children. Three years later, he commissioned the construction of an 8,200-sq. foot Spanish Colonial Revival-style mansion that overlooks Lake Como.

In 1933, Sealy sold the lavish home to Maco Stewart, a prominent businessman from a wealthy family. He graduated from the University of Texas with a law degree. He founded the Stewart Title Company of Texas, where he served for many years as the company's president. Soon after purchasing the mansion, Stewart began expanding.

Stewart married three times and had two children before his death in 1950. Urban legend told stories of Stewart killing his family and burying them in the mansion's walls, but this can be proven false. The University of Texas Medical Branch was the final owner of the estate. They operated the building as a home for sick and disabled children. They maintained ownership until the property began to show its age and fell to decay.

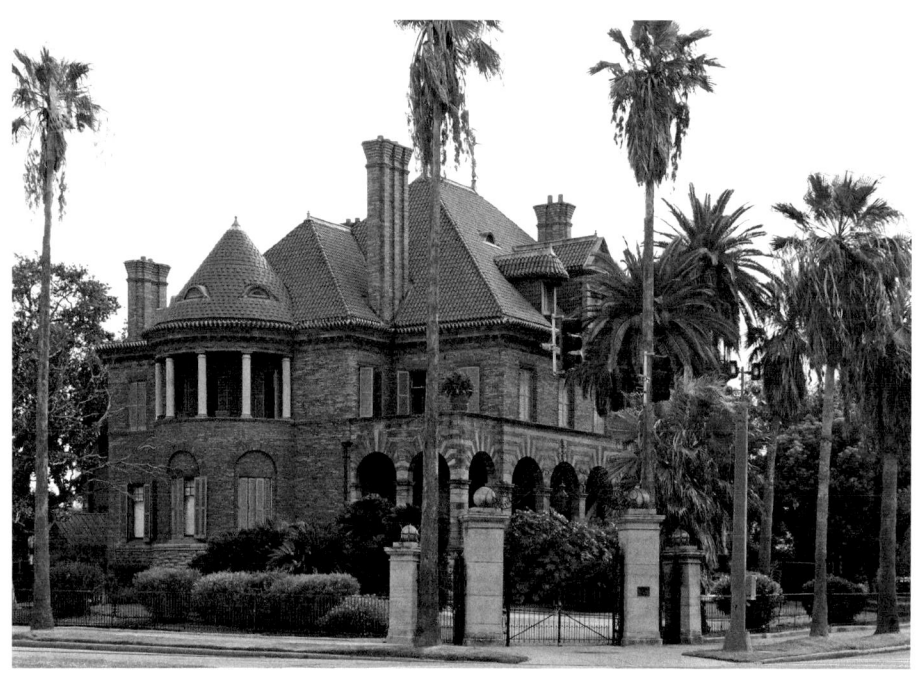
A majestic gate blocks the entrance to the historic home. (*Michael Barera*)

The Stewart mansion officially entered an abandoned state in 1968. As with any old, creepy, abandoned mansion, rumors of hauntings filled the air. At the same time, I attempted to place validity behind the accusations. Validation required me to start at the base.

The land on which the mansion stands formally gave home to the indigenous tribe of the Karankawa, who concentrated along the Gulf of Mexico and the coastal regions of Southern Texas. Historical research on the Karankawa is limited and hindered by tribe enemies documenting false information. Some historians believe the Karankawa received a bad rap as cannibals due to their enemies. However, others argue that tribes along the coast of Texas and Louisiana did partake in this odd custom, and the Karankawa were likely to follow suit. Regardless, indigenous people hold a high value on spiritual beliefs and proper regard for their ancestors. Often settlers neglected grave markers and possible sacred burial grounds.

Pirate Jean Lafitte spent time on the Galveston beaches, and in 1817, he founded a new colony on Galveston Island called Campeche. Speaking French, English, and some Spanish, Lafitte is described as handsome and having aristocratic manners. However, the Karankawa occupied land which he acquired. Lafitte's men did what pirates do and kidnapped Karankawa women. Her tribe retaliated by killing five of

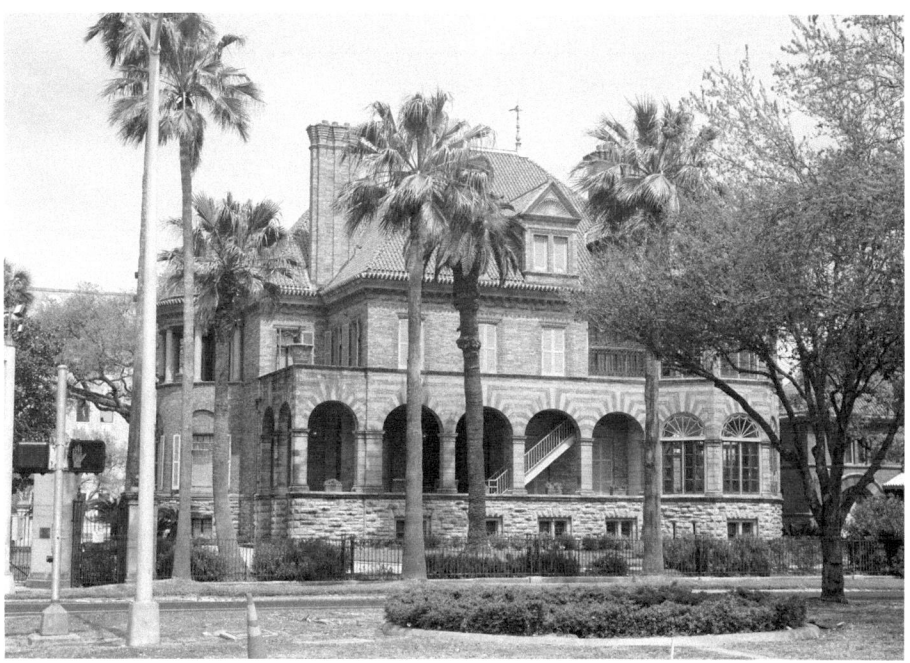

Tall palms surround the Stewart mansion. (*Michael Barera*)

Lafitte's men. The battle continued, and Lafitte's men killed most Karankawa men in 1821 during a conflict known as the Battle of Three Trees, which lasted only three days. Murals inside the mansion show pirates fighting and standing proud as if the spirit of Lafitte himself inspired the beautiful paintings.

Over the years, caretakers at Stewart mansion have reported seeing pirates and Karankawa warriors sneaking around corners. They have heard cannon fire, gunfire, and screaming. Doors slammed on their own accord. Lafitte buried a treasure chest near the mansion, but visitors fear it is not the only item lingering at the mansion door. Disembodied voices and footsteps remain through the empty halls.

## PEARLAND MANSION

In 2001, Dr. Ulysses "Sonny" Watkins and his wife supervised the construction of two mansions. Builders designed the first building as a post-surgical rehabilitation center with an astounding 64,000 sq. feet. The enormous mansion featured forty-six bedrooms and fifty-five bathrooms, an indoor swimming pool, a sauna, an elevator, and a nine-car garage. The second home measures 32,000 sq. feet and served as a home for the doctor and his wife. Both mansions remained empty, and even the most prominent structure was left uncompleted.

Locals call the estates the Manvel Mansions and say they are under reconstruction for a church and school. However, it sat abandoned for almost fifteen years and haunted the town residents by sitting alone in a 15-acre lot.

Jim Youngblood, the current owner, stated in an interview with ABC13, "Many people in the area believe the house is haunted."

In 2017 the mansion was to be transformed into a residential facility for at-risk military veterans. However, even the United States government had trouble finding the funding to repair the damages of time and vandals. This plan did not succeed, but there are high hopes as Youngblood begins to rent out spaces and complete the restoration. As the school and church move in, they might calm the uneasy spirits of the abandoned halls.

## Ashton Villa

James Brown was a hardware businessman and prominent banker who moved to Galveston, Texas, in 1843. He influenced the building of the first brick jail and a general store. Brown was a member of the first volunteer fire brigade, which was organized in 1843.

In 1846, he married Rebecca Stoddart and prepared to start his family. This same year, Brown became Galveston, Houston and Henderson Railroad president. Brown was ready to settle down and make his home in Galveston. It was with family in mind that Brown began construction on what would become the first brick-constructed home in Galveston. The three-story Italian-style structure became known as Ashton Villa to honor Rebecca's ancestor, Lieutenant Isaac Ashton, a Revolutionary War hero.

Brown received an honorary title of colonel during the Civil War when he helped transport men from Houston to recapture Galveston from Union troops. Ashton Villa also served as a hospital and haven for the Confederate soldiers and headquarters for both sides of the war.

Brown died on December 24, 1895. His widow and five children remained safe during the hurricane of 1900 inside the thick brick walls of Ashton Villa. The hurricane filled the basement with sand and silt from the Gulf, and the surrounding grounds gained about 2 feet of fresh dirt. Rebecca Brown lived at Ashton Villa until her death.

In 1927, a granddaughter of the Brown family sold the villa to El Mina Shrine. The Shriners made minor modifications but used the estate for nearly forty years as their business offices and social functions. In June 1986, they placed the property for sale.

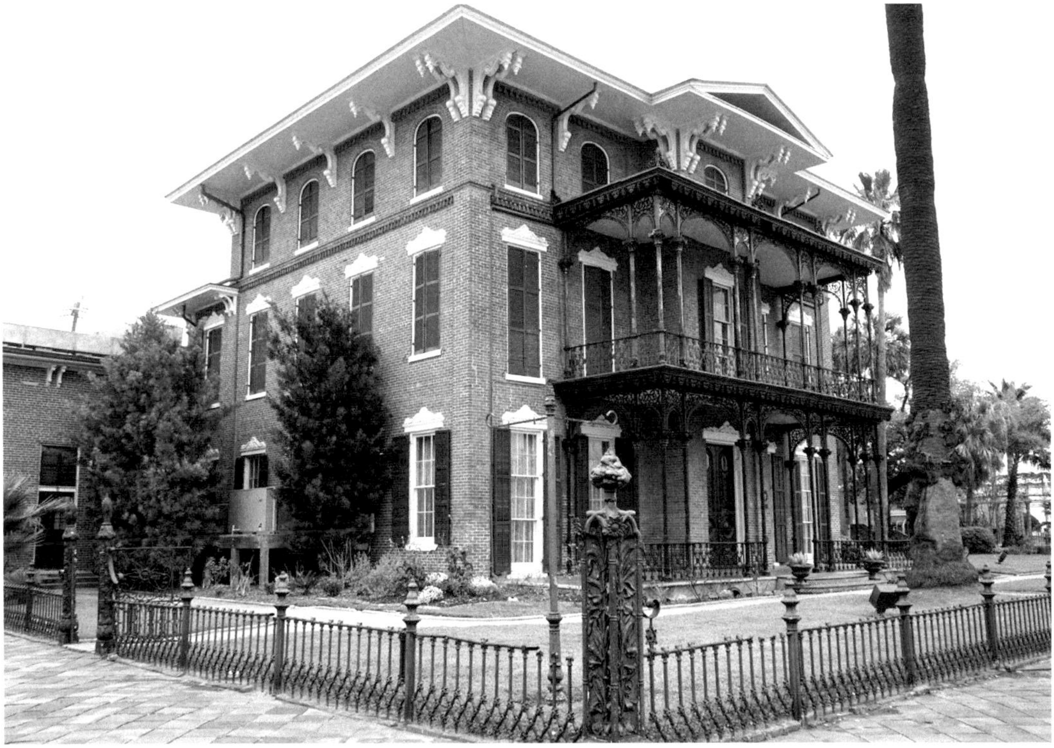

A fence and gate enclose Ashton Villa. (*Carol Highsmith*)

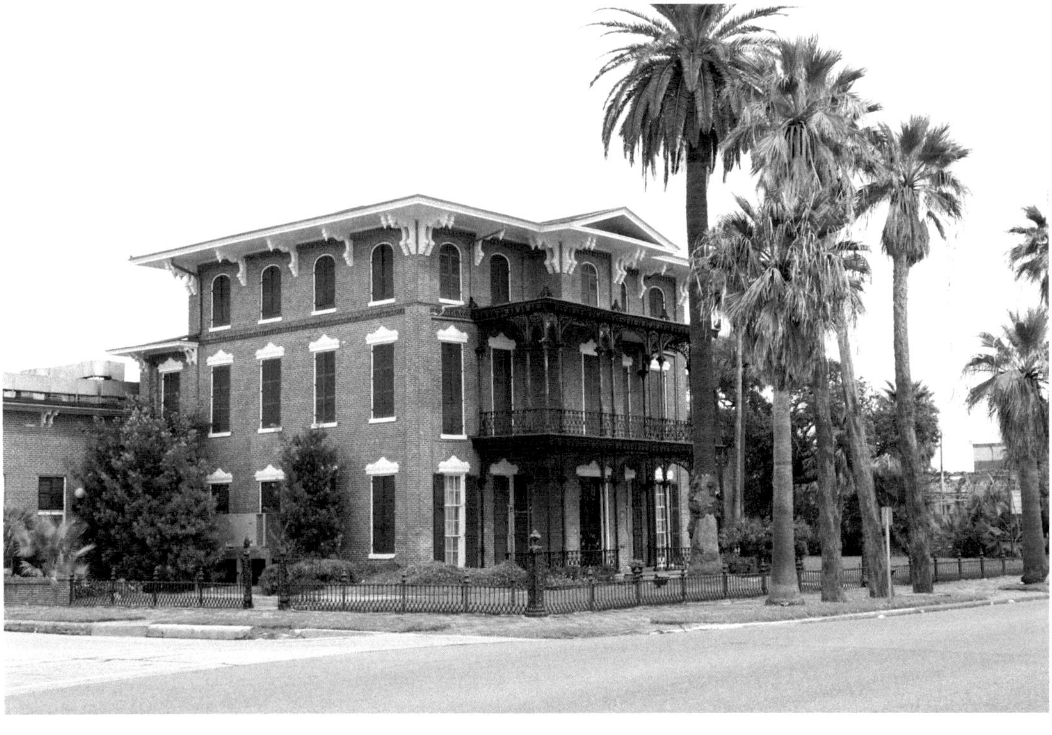

Tall palms tree tower over the large home. (*Carol Highsmith*)

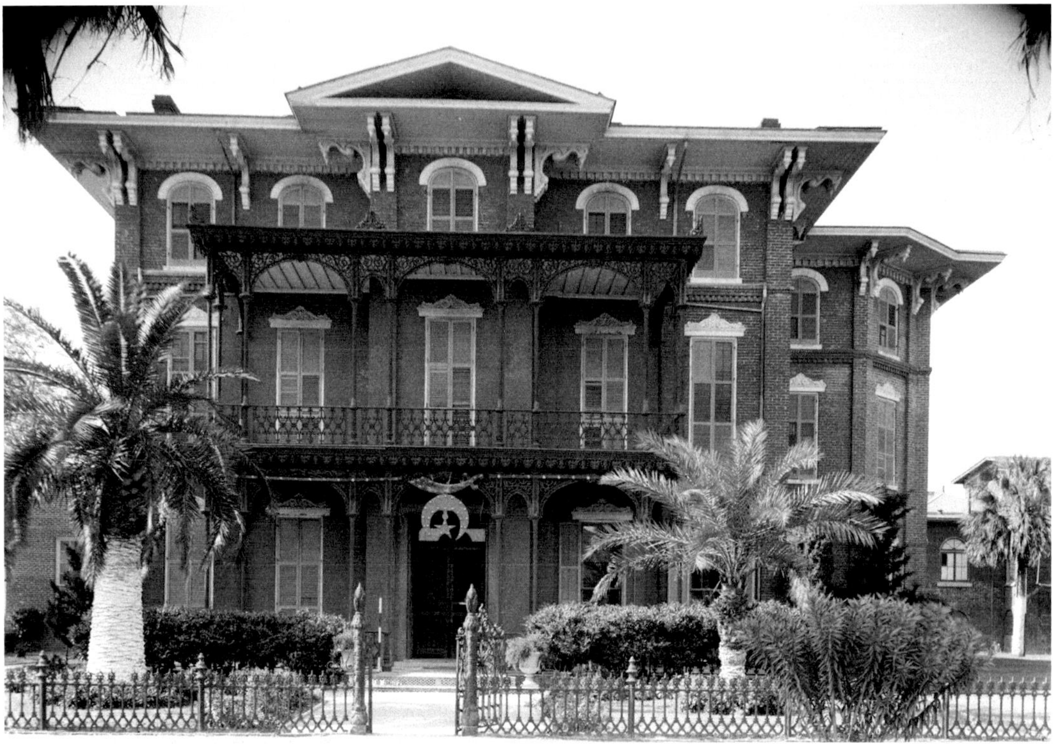

The overall feel of Ashton Villa is exquisite. (*Jas. I. Campbell*)

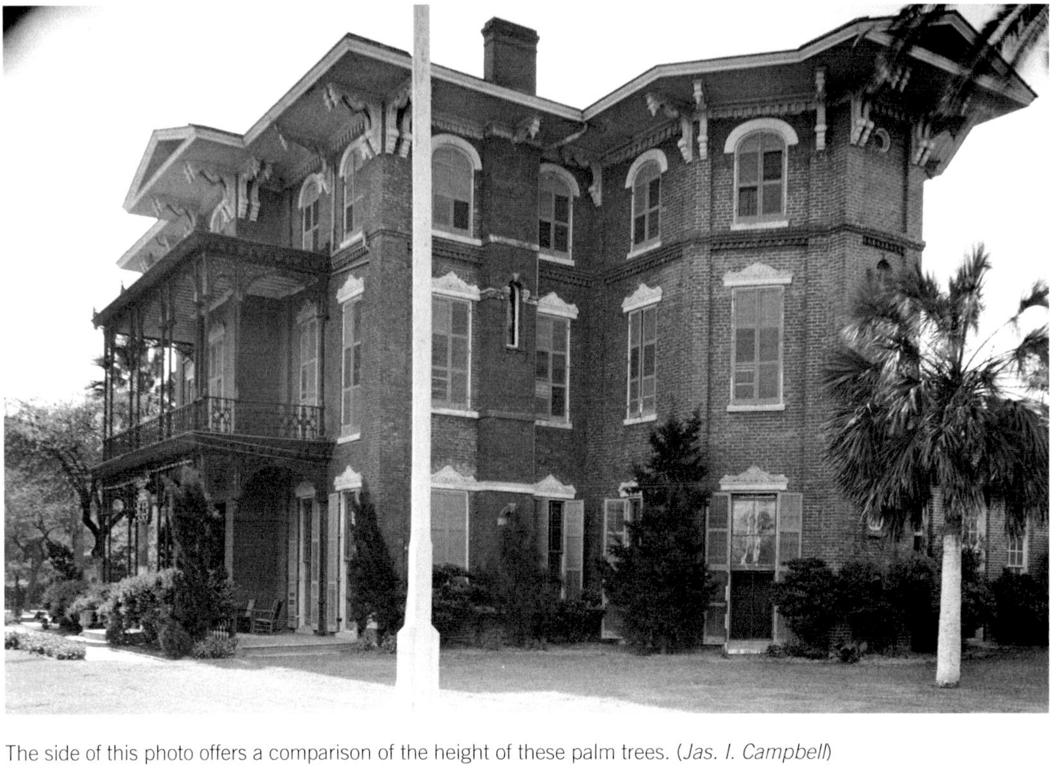

The side of this photo offers a comparison of the height of these palm trees. (*Jas. I. Campbell*)

Two spirits haunting Ashton Villa are said to be Bettie and Tilly Brown, the daughters of James Brown.

Bettie Brown earned the nickname "The Texas Princess" as her parents raised her in an atmosphere of extravagance and privilege. Bettie had a bit of a rebellious attitude. She liked to race carriages down the streets, smoke cigars in public, and travel without a chaperone. Bettie traveled to Egypt, India, Jerusalem, and even Morocco on her own. She also enjoyed hosting lavish parties. Visitors claim to see her in the Gold Room or at the top of the stairs. During a tour, a guide witnessed an apparition at the second-floor landing. The ghost was dressed in a lavish ballgown and held a detailed fan in her hand, which had been one of Bettie's belongings. The chests of drawers in Bettie's room tend to lock and unlock with no assistance, and sometimes the keys disappear entirely. A former manager claimed to see the ceiling fans turn themselves off and on and continue to spin with the switch in the off position. The fans and the alarm going off happened on February 18, 1991, Bettie's birthday. Bettie crafts several of the more risqué paintings in the mansion. Perhaps she is drawn to the objects she invested a tremendous amount of time and love in.

Tilly married in 1884. Many believe her husband was abusive to Tilly and their children. Maids and family members testified to the abuse during their divorce. The courts denied Tilly's husband the home and custody of their children. Ashton Villa was a respite for the sweet, kind-hearted woman during her divorce. Ten years after the divorce, her husband died. A caretaker awoke to the slight sound of a piano playing. Tilly played piano. The caretaker identified a female apparition but could not say if it was Tilly. The Galveston Historical Society notes that Tilly played both violin and piano.

A disembodied male voice vibrates around the estate. He argues with an unseen woman and appears angry. Some suspect this to be the spirit of Tilly's husband returning for his vengeance and to get in the last word.

Many soldiers entered the doors as the estate served as a makeshift hospital during the Civil War. General Gordon Granger is said to have announced the war's end on the villa's veranda.

## Bishop's Palace or Gresham House

This home is well known as both Bishop's Palace and Gresham House and is a three-story masonry mansion with a partially raised basement. It is constructed primarily of limestone, a known conductor of paranormal activity, and resembles a castle. The front entrance is a grand flight of stone steps.

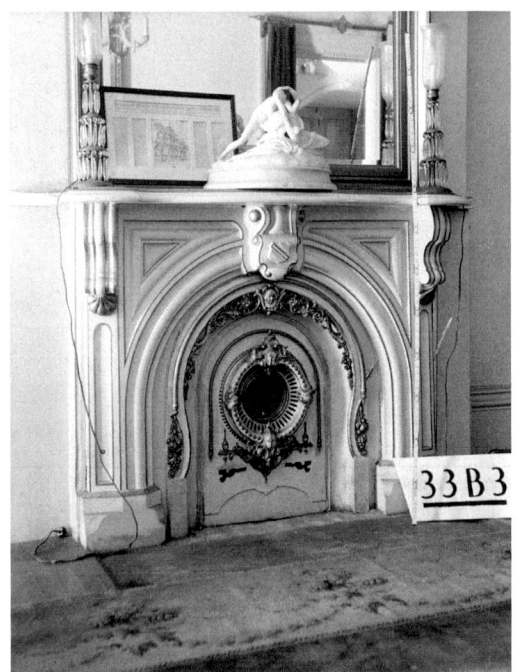 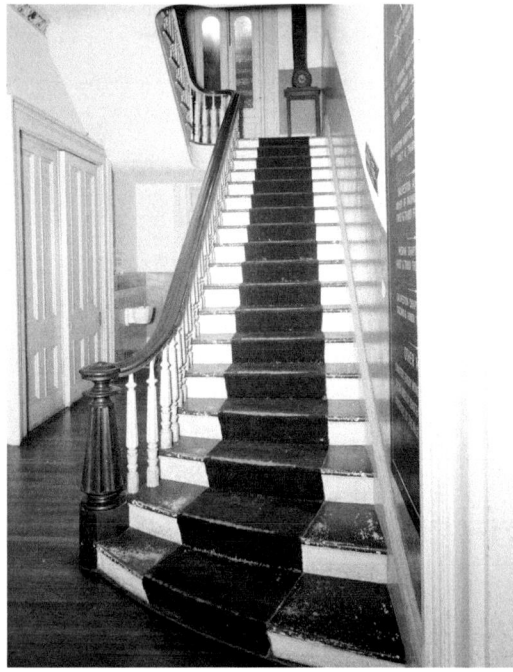

*Above left:* The fireplace is marked with soot, which is adds an eerie feel to the scene. (*Jas. I. Campbell*)

*Above right:* Carpeted staircases adorn the home between floors. (*Jas. I. Campbell*)

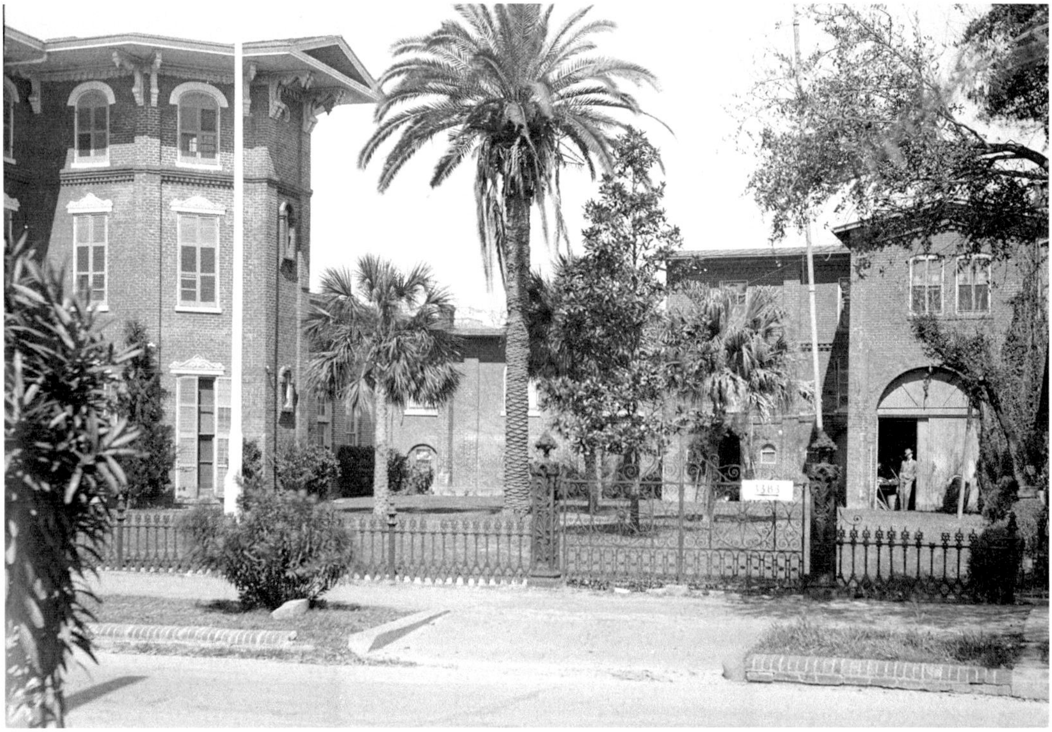

A carriage house sits next door to Ashton Villa. (*Jas. I. Campbell*)

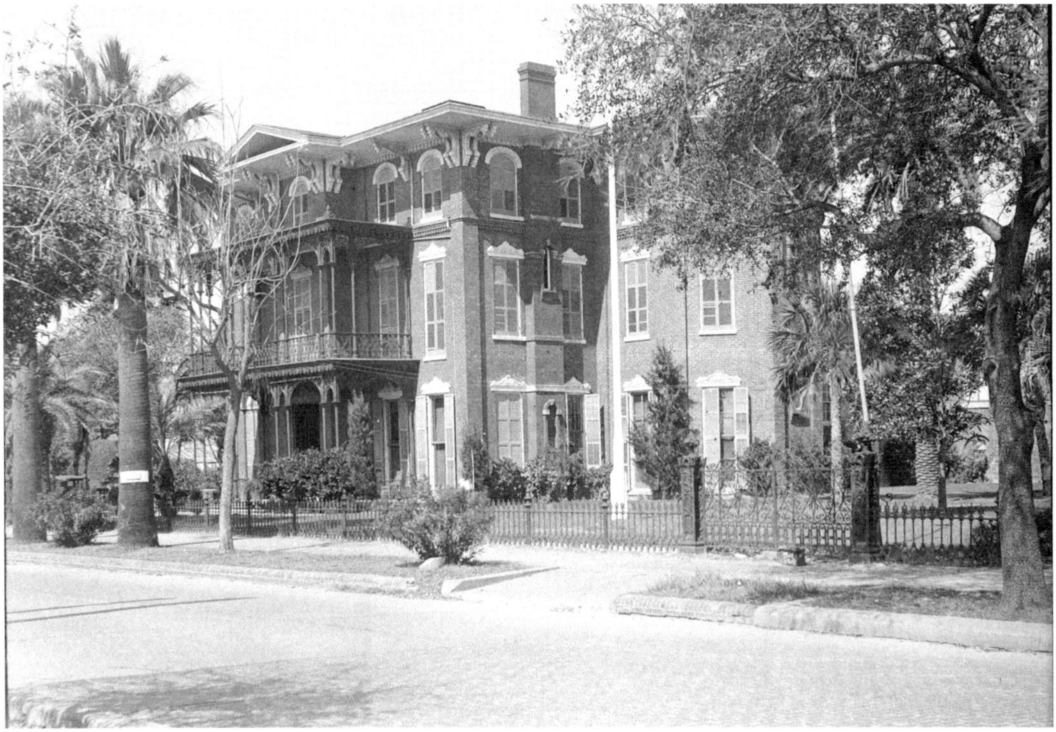

The palm-lined street offers a tropical feel. (*Jas. I. Campbell*)

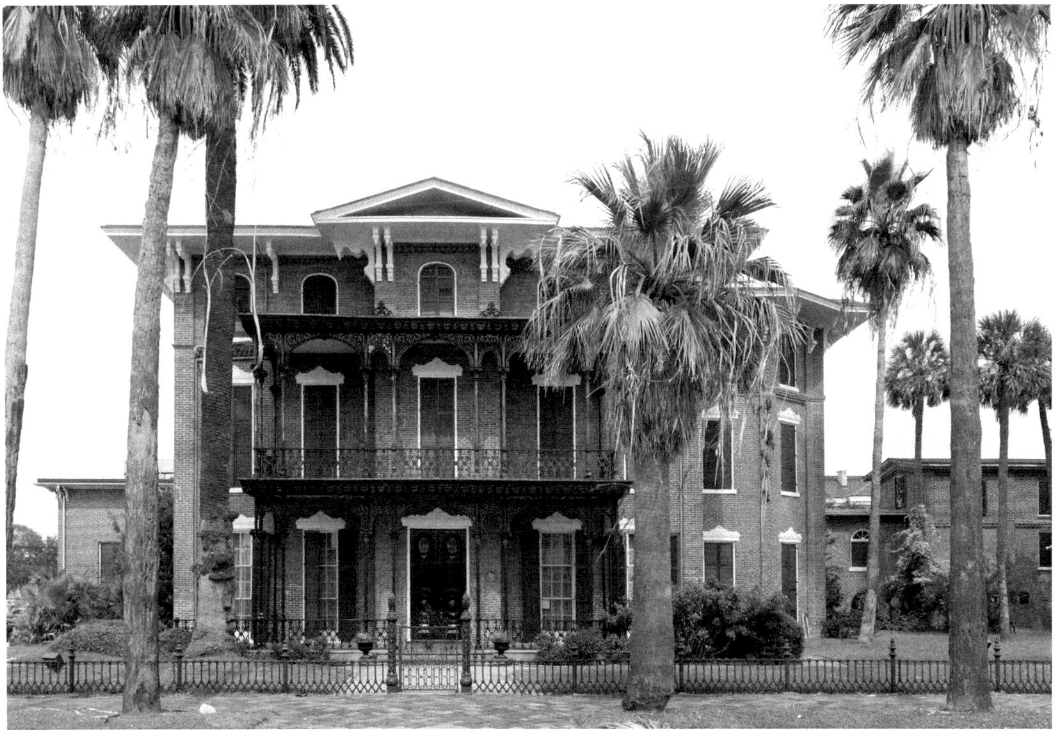

Ashton Villa is located in the heart of Galveston's historic district. (*Carol Highsmith*)

It was built by Walter Gresham, a prominent lawyer, Texas legislator, and representative to the fifty-third Congress. Despite his parents being prominent lawyers and attending private schools from an early age, the war depleted his family fortune when Gresham moved to Texas in 1866. He had $5 in his pocket. Gresham opened a law office in 1886 and married Josephine Mann. With time and career advancements, Gresham began to reclaim the family fortune.

In 1887, plans for Gresham House began when Gresham commissioned architect Nicholas Clayton to design the home. Construction began later that year and took six years to complete. They formally opened their home on January 1, 1893. After the hurricane of 1900, the Greshams opened their door to hundreds of survivors. This hurricane was catastrophic for Galveston Island, killing nearly 8,000 residents.

In 1923, the Greshams sold their home to the Galveston-Houston Diocese of the Catholic church. The castle became home to the Most Reverend Christopher Byrne. At this time, the house became known as Bishop's Palace. He lived there until April 1, 1950, when he died from a heart attack. His body returned to the home because he passed on a Saturday. His body remains in the castle until Monday evening. The following day, his body lay in state at the cathedral.

After the Most-Reverend Byrne, the castle housed the Most-Reverend Vincent Harris. In 1963, the Catholic church turned the home over to the Newman Club, and three months later, it became open to the public but abandoned by a permeant occupant.

Some may find a 19,082-sq. foot castle with an eclectic architectural design to be mysterious. Those who have visited the castle have other reasons to see it eerie. There are reports of pushing, scratching, tripping, and even punching from invisible forces within the castle walls. These behaviors do not appear fitting for Gresham or his wife, nor do they include the actions of a bishop. Could this be the hurricane victims racing for refuge?

Walter and Josephine Gresham may have returned to their first home to protect the structure. Their presence arrived when the castle was undergoing renovations. Walter likes to roam the halls and becomes most active during hurricane season. During bad weather, he nervously wanders and paces back and forth on the front porch. Josephine likes to keep an eye on her card box. This particular box contained relics from her travels. Josephine always sent postcards home when she traveled. Some reports say the box moves without visible assistance.

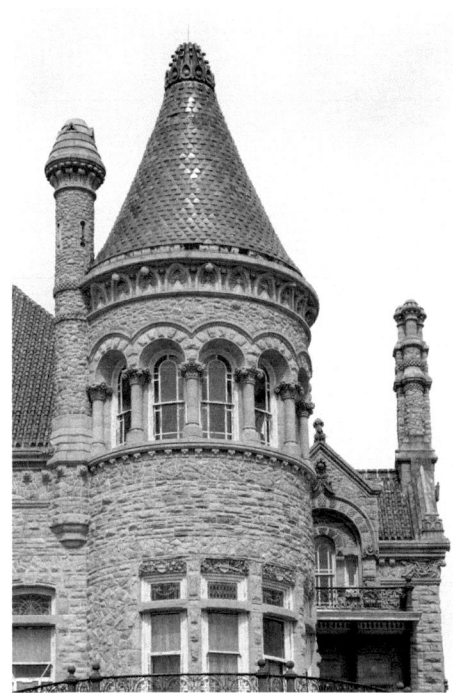

*Right:* Bishop's palace looks more like a castle than a home. (*Carol Highsmith*)

*Below:* Tall turrets reach the sky. (*Carol Highsmith*)

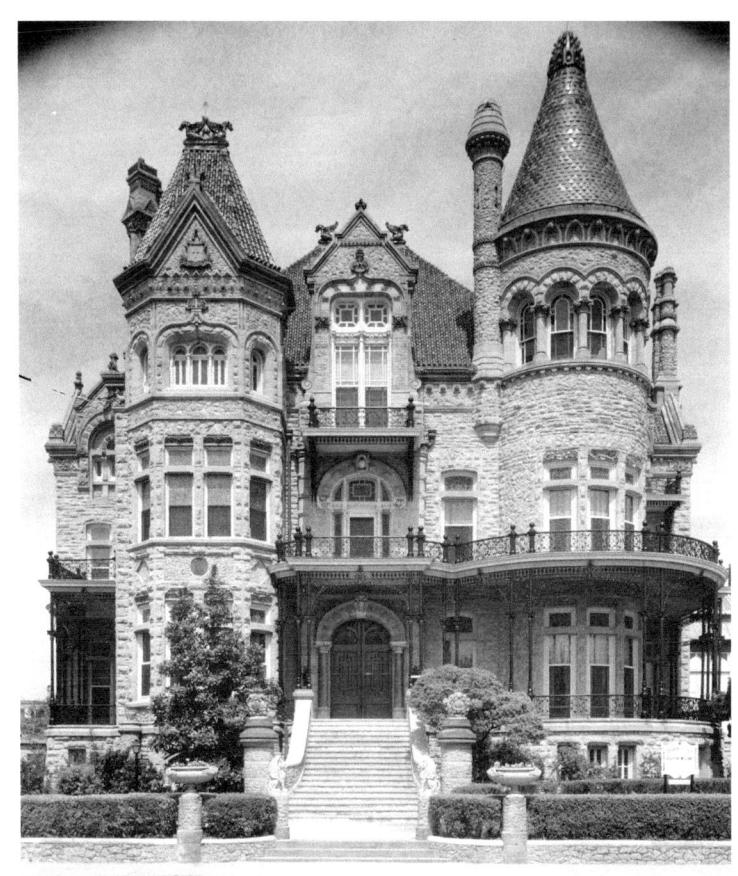

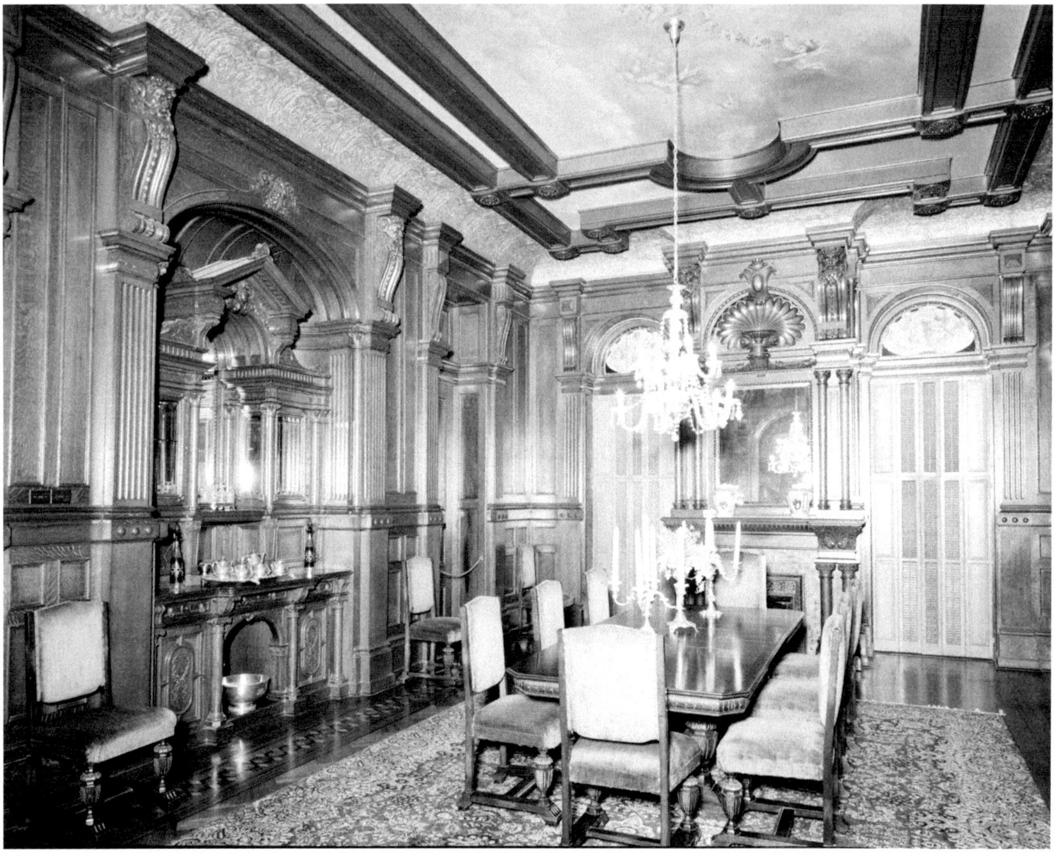

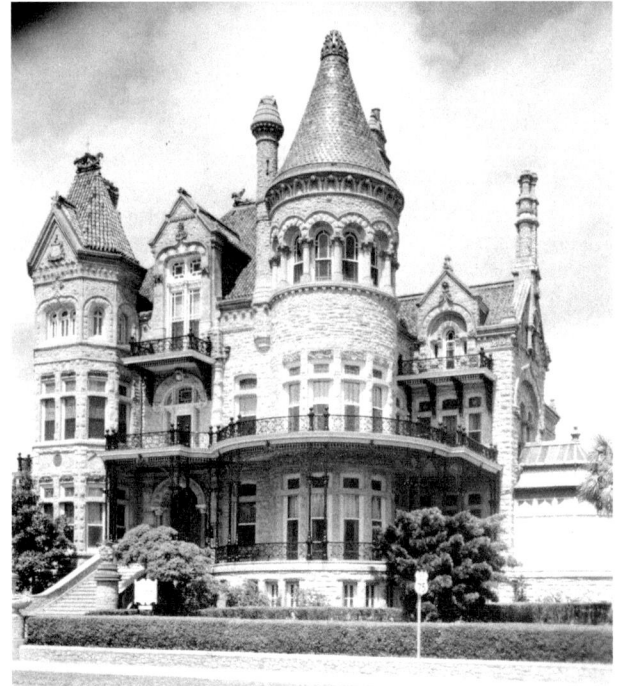

*Above:* The regal dining area is fit for a king or a bishop. (*Carol Highsmith*)

*Left:* During the hurricane in the early 1900s, many locals came to seek shelter at the mansion. (*Carol Highsmith*)

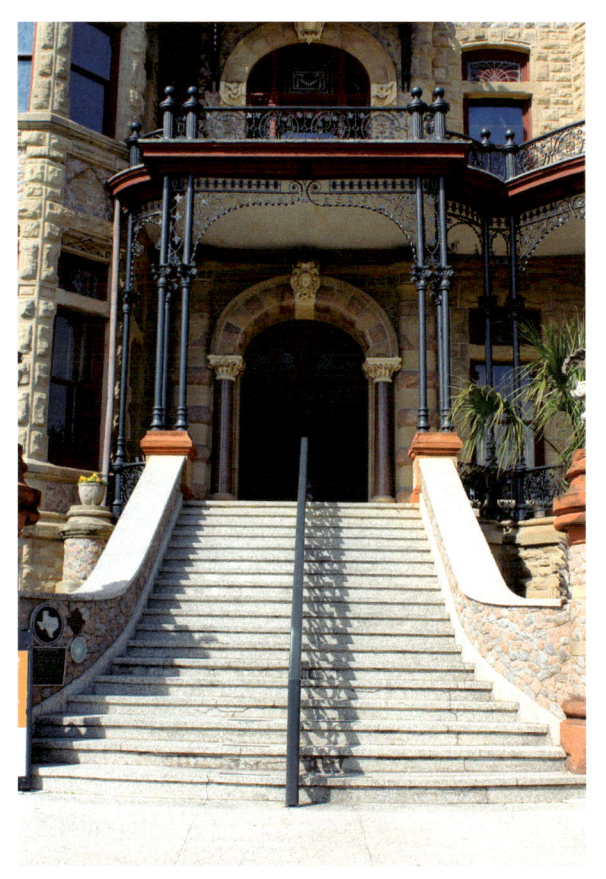

Majestic, concrete stairs lead to the entrance of the Bishop's palace. (*Farragutful*)

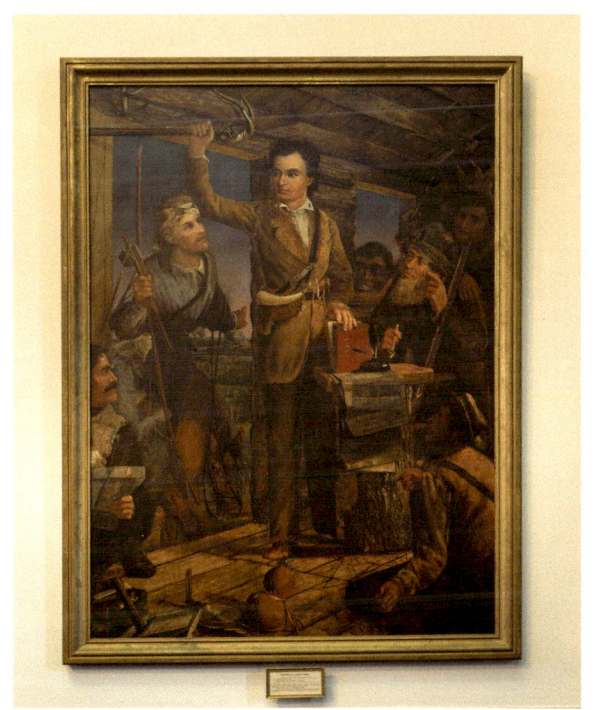

French pirate Jean Lafitte poses for a painting. (*Library of Congress*)

# The Grove

This Greek Revival-style home is in Jefferson, Texas, and underwent construction in 1861. The single-story, wood-framed house forms a modified L-plan with weatherboard siding. It sits on a half-acre lot of lush vegetation and some of the state's oldest pecan trees, dating back over 130 years. An English-style garden with a brick path hosts day lilies and tiger lilies planted by Daphne Young, who owned the property with her husband Charles from 1885–1955.

Frank Stilley, a cotton merchant, originally built the home in a simple square plan with a parlor, dining room, and two bedrooms for him and his wife. The kitchen itself was external and down a short walkway from home. In 1870, works combined the kitchen with the original structure. Stilley was a respected businessman. Some say his fate lay in an arranged marriage, but others say he developed a romantic relationship with his wife, Minerva, through the years. Minerva's father financed the cost of the home. With a simple yet delicate design, the home showed the general public the success of the cotton farmer. Some area maps began referring to the location as "Mr. Stilley's house in the grove" or "The Rock's house in the grove." The name became shortened to "The Grove." The couple resided at The Grove until 1880, when Minerva died after battling a long illness. Frank sold the home to Daniel and Amanda Rock.

The second owner was a bridge builder who helped turn Jefferson into an inland port. The third owners, Charles and Daphne Young, an African American couple, were the longest residents at home, and gardens flourished under Daphne's green thumb. Charles Young passed away in December 1938 at eighty years of age. The final renovations were completed in 1939 after Young died and left the house to his wife and daughters. When Daphne passed away, the couple's daughter Louise lived in the house until 1983. Louise's estate sold the home to Colonel Daniel and Lucile Grove. The Groves held the property for only eight years before Colonel Grove passed away and his wife sold the property.

In 1991, a chef named Patrick Hopkins purchased the property to open a restaurant called The Grove. The restaurant closed in 1998, and the home sat abandoned for four years. The current owners, Mitchel and Tami Whitington, purchased the house in 2002.

The first ghost stories spread when Louise Young lived alone in the home. At first, she bragged to friends about the haunts, but later she became terrified of the ghosts. Louise installed extra exterior lights to deter visitors from walking the garden at night. When she would see a shadow, she turned on the lights, and the figure disappeared. As years passed, there were reports to the police about intruders in the home. However, when deputies arrived, there were no human intruders.

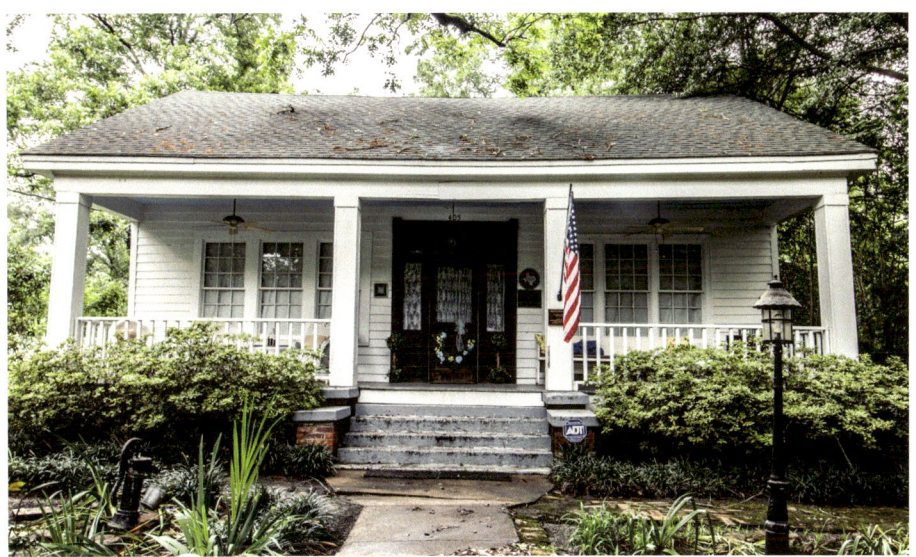

*Above:* The home was built in 1891 by Frank and Minerva Stilley. (*National Historic Register*)

*Below:* A brick walkway connects the home to the driveway and garden cottage. (*National Historic Register*)

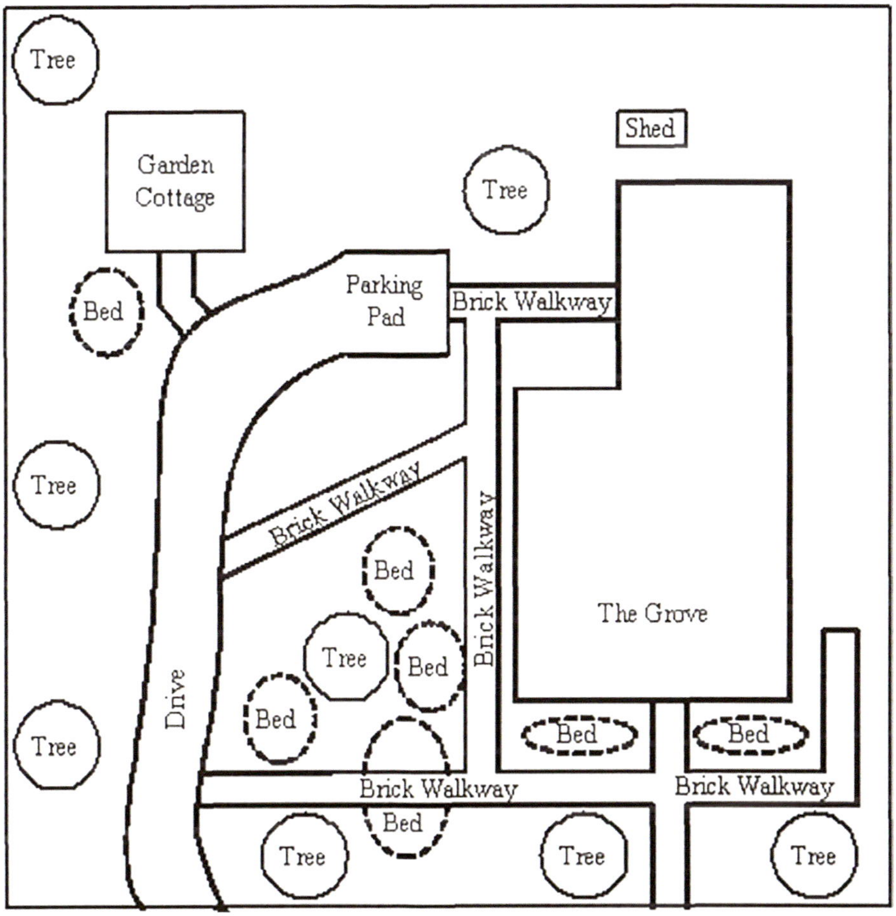

Another story tells of Mrs. Grove, who awakened one night to a dark, ominous mass engulfing the room. She was said to have taken her bible to bed every night to pray.

Patrick Hopkins reports he witnessed someone walk down the hall to the bathroom but never come out. Another staff member claimed a dog attacked her, but no one saw a dog.

Disembodied voices, footsteps, a feeling of being watched, mysterious wet spots, and loud wails plague the home, often called one of the most haunted locations in Texas. The current owners state that paranormal events occur but do not feel scared or threatened. They think former owners may return to visit a home they once loved. They have seen a happy man walking through the house in a dark suit and top hat and a woman in a white dress. They have seen many small, dark shadows. They are not smokers but have smelt cigar smoke at times. A man with a long, white beard shows up with a gun to protect the home when no one is around.

## Walnut Ridge Mansion

James Miller moved to Texas with his parents in 1845. He was a teacher by the age of nineteen and studied law. He passed the bar in 1854 and practiced before the Texas Supreme Court a year later.

After the war, he returned to Gonzalez to practice law. He remarried on May 10, 1868, to Julia Batchelor. The same year, he retired from his law practice, partnered with William Sayers, and founded a bank in Gonzalez. Miller became the first president of the Texas Bankers Association. He experimented with raising cattle, primarily Durham, Holstein, and Jersey cows. He became so good at raising cattle that he served as the first Texas Live Stock Association president.

Miller was the Grand Master of Masons in 1873. He was the Grand Commander of the Knights Templar of Texas. In 1883, Miller was elected as a Democrat to the 48th and 49th Congresses and served until 1887. He declined a renomination to the 50th Congress to return his focus to his business. Two days before his death, Miller fell ill but was unaware of the gravity of his condition. He passed away on July 3, 1902. His cause of death was determined to be congestion of the kidneys. Miller passed away in his home, which he named Walnut Ridge.

J. Riley Gordon, a renowned architect famous for designing fifteen courthouses across Texas, was selected to design Walnut Ridge for Miller. The Greek Revival-style mansion reached completion in 1901. When Miller passed away the following year, his widow Julia, remained in the home. The couple did not have children. After a long battle with an illness, Julia passed away in her home on April 15, 1912. While

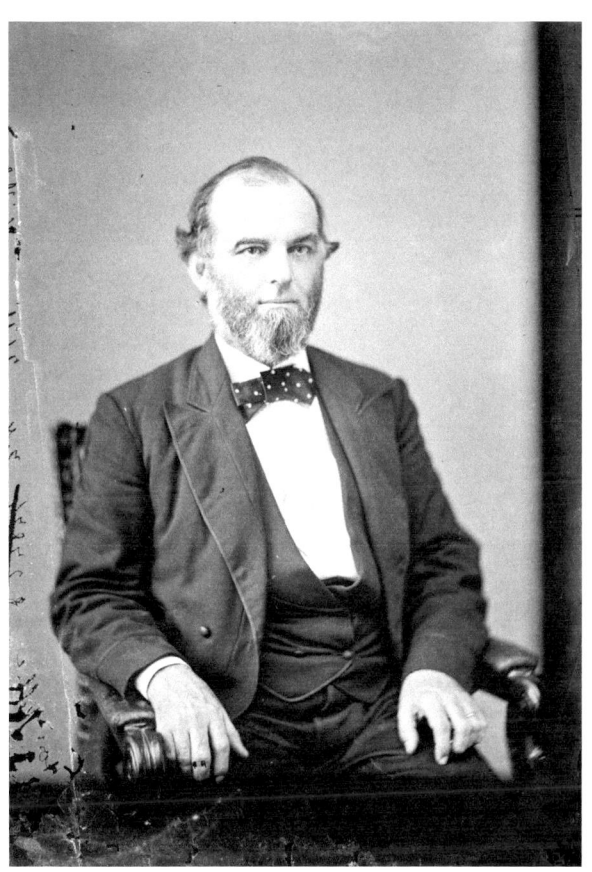

James Francis Miller poses for a formal portrait. (*Library of Congress*)

the couple had less than a year together in the majestic home, they may have found a way to spend eternity together.

The home passed through many various owners before becoming abandoned. TSG Architects of Gonzalez has begun a restoration of the once glorious mansion and hopes to restore Walnut Ridge to its previous splendor to preserve this vital piece of history.

# 2

# BOOS BEHIND BARS

## Frio County Jail

Aaron Oden laid out the town of Frio in 1871, and it became the county seat that same year. The townsite included the Frio River in an area that was low and easy to cross. Dempsey Forrest built the stone jail, and before completion, voters requested that the upper story construction was of stone instead of wood. This upper floor served as a jury room. Over the years, many notorious characters spent time at the Frio County Jail. Sam Bass, Jesse, and Frank James spent time locked down in Frio for minor crimes. The jail foundation sat 3 feet in the ground, and the walls were to be 3 feet thick and built of hard stone. The floors featured flagstone at least 4 inches thick. The cell windows were iron, and the doors held 0.5 × 3-inch-wide iron bars.

The town constructed the courthouse and post office in 1872. Sadly in 1877, the courthouse burned to the ground. Local rancher William Slaughter assisted in the construction of a new stone courthouse at his own expense.

Frio was an outpost of civilization surrounded by tribes of hostile Comanches. The population waxed and waned as people seeking a haven from the Comanche attacks came into town for shelter. The first grace in Frio belongs to Calvin Massey, whom the Comanches killed in the spring of 1873. Frio had a population of around 1,500 and continued to thrive. However, that ceased when the railroad bypassed the Frio River in 1881. The county seat, the business, and most citizens moved to Pearsall by 1883. Frio city was back to being just a tiny town. The courthouse became a general store and post office combined. By 1890, only 100 people remain in the city. Today, only the abandoned courthouse, jail, and cemetery remain.

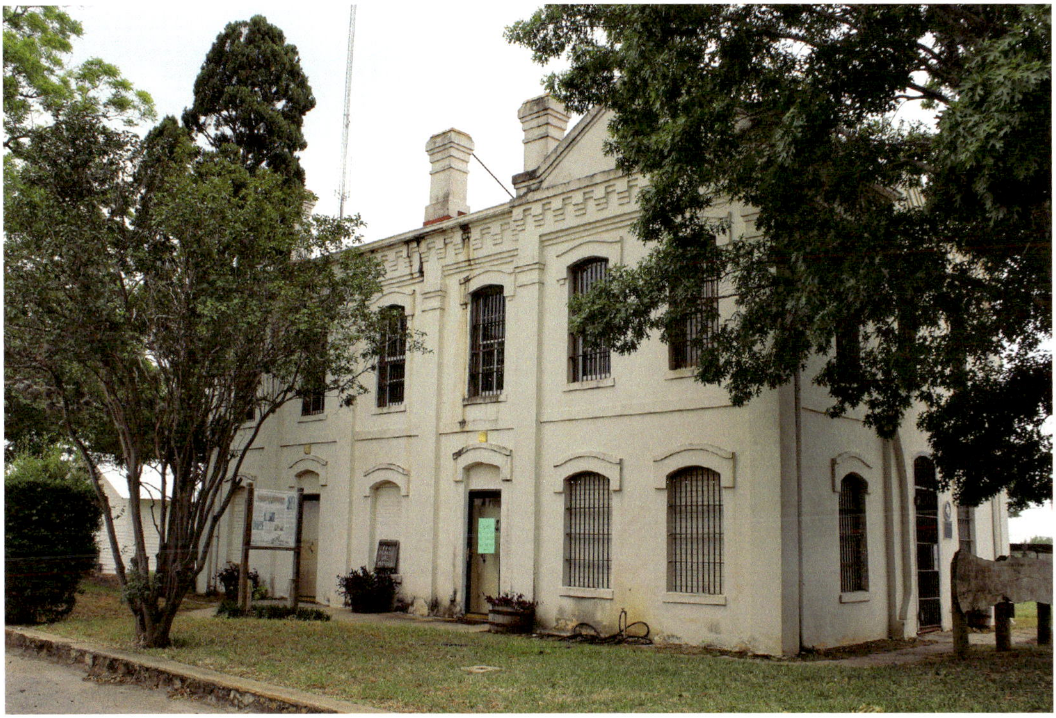

*Above:* The white stone exterior of the jail is ghostly. (*Darryl Pearson*)

*Right:* A sign commemorates the construction and life of this old building. (*Darryl Pearson*)

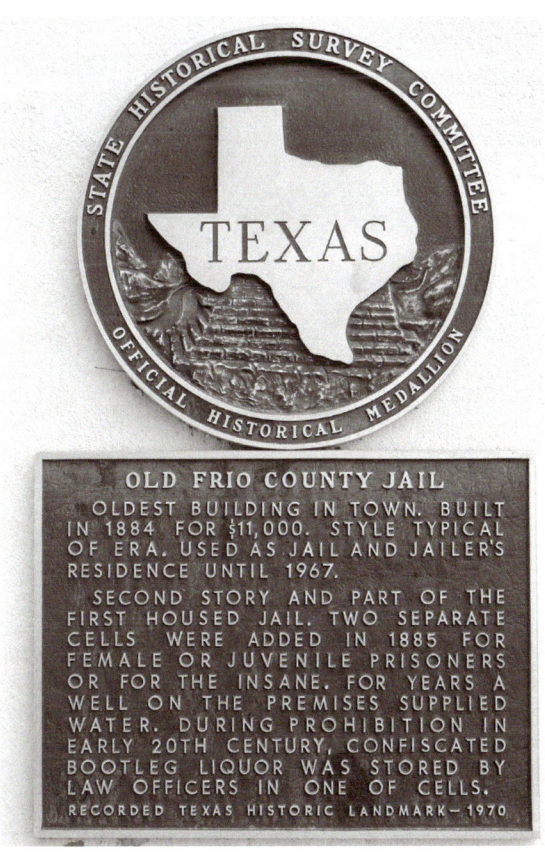

**OLD FRIO COUNTY JAIL**
OLDEST BUILDING IN TOWN. BUILT IN 1884 FOR $11,000. STYLE TYPICAL OF ERA. USED AS JAIL AND JAILER'S RESIDENCE UNTIL 1967.
SECOND STORY AND PART OF THE FIRST HOUSED JAIL. TWO SEPARATE CELLS WERE ADDED IN 1885 FOR FEMALE OR JUVENILE PRISONERS OR FOR THE INSANE. FOR YEARS A WELL ON THE PREMISES SUPPLIED WATER. DURING PROHIBITION IN EARLY 20TH CENTURY, CONFISCATED BOOTLEG LIQUOR WAS STORED BY LAW OFFICERS IN ONE OF CELLS.
RECORDED TEXAS HISTORIC LANDMARK — 1970

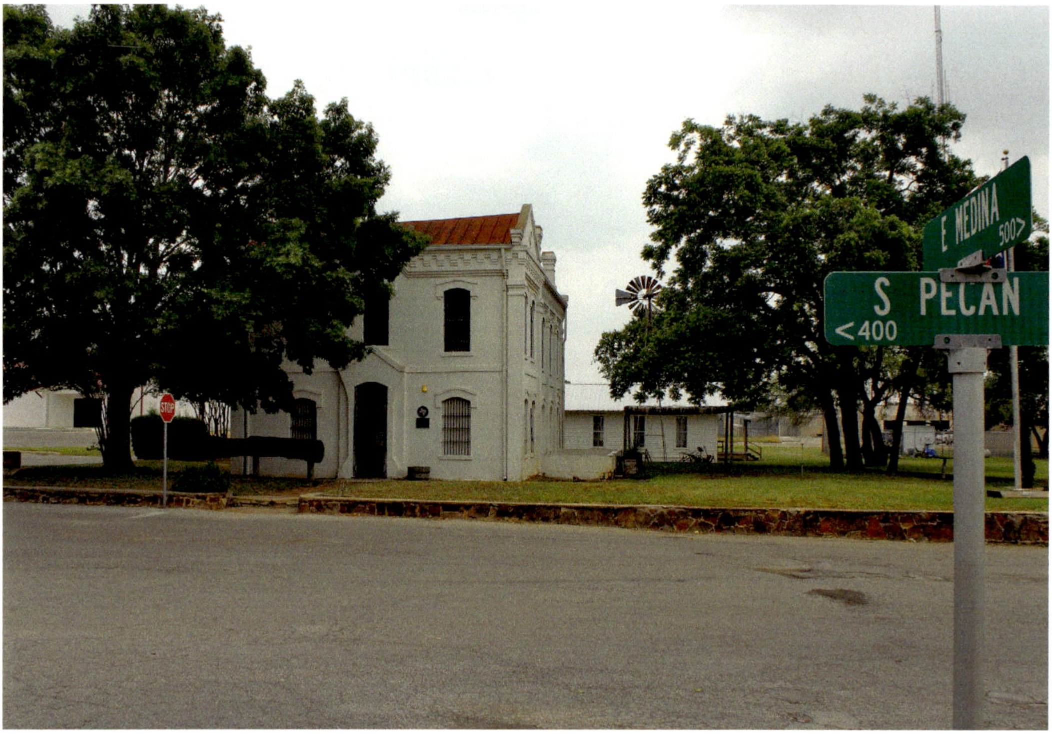

It is almost impossible to tell this building housed outlaws from the outside. (*Darryl Pearson*)

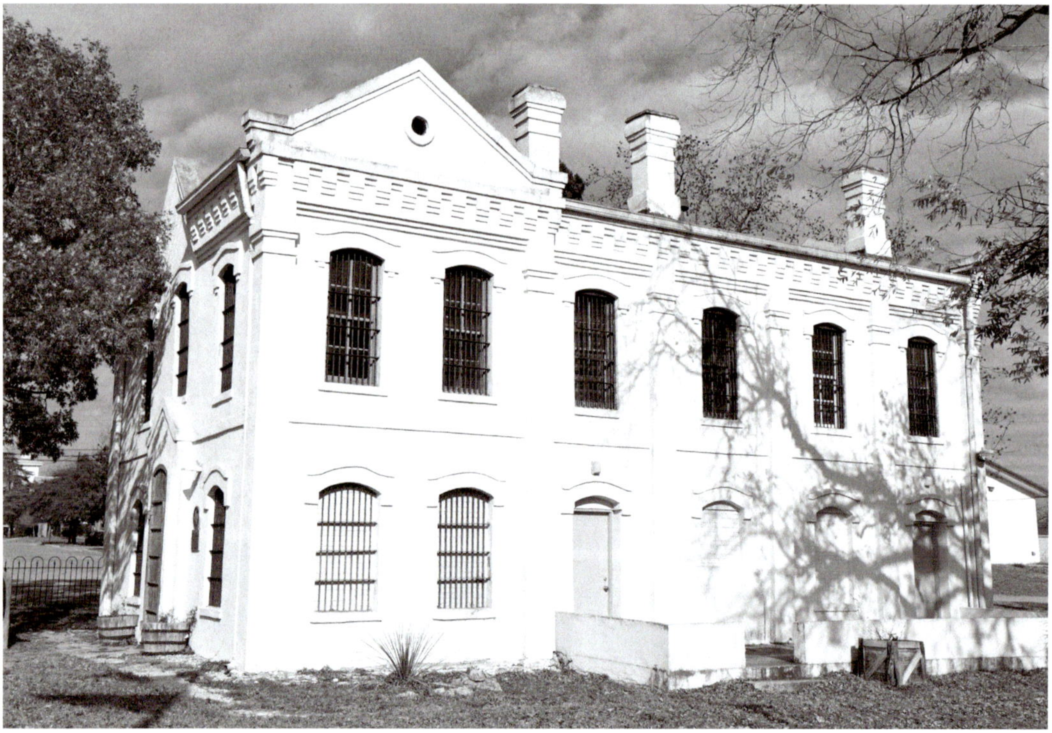

Bars cover the windows on both floors to prevent anyone from escaping. (*Billy Hawthorn*)

The Frio River is said to be haunted by a woman in white. She manifests as a wisp of fog and develops into a woman wearing a white dress. Some believe she is Maria Juarez. Maria lived with her sister, who married a handsome man named Gregorio. Maria was the youngest sister and helped around the house and assisted with caring for her nieces and nephews in exchange for living in the home. Gregorio noticed how beautiful she was becoming as she aged and developed an interest in his wife's sister. Maria did not have feelings for Gregorio and went on to develop a relationship with another cowboy, Anselmo Tobar. Maria longed to be married and have children like her sister and hoped Tobar would propose. He eventually did, and Maria began planning her big day. The wedding plans irritated Gregorio. He intended to win Maria over and prevent her from marrying anyone else.

One fateful day, Gregorio confessed his love to Maria. She shut him down flat and ran home, waiting for Tobar to visit so she could tell him about the incident. Later that night, Maria heard a noise and went outside to meet him, believing it was Tobar. She ran into Gregorio, who drew his pistol and fatally shot Maria directly in her heart. Gregorio ran away but was eventually caught, tried, and held prisoner. Maria's sister prepared her body for burial. She used the beautiful white wedding gown Maria had hoped to wear when she married Tobar. She braided her long, luxurious hair and laced it with white ribbons and wildflowers.

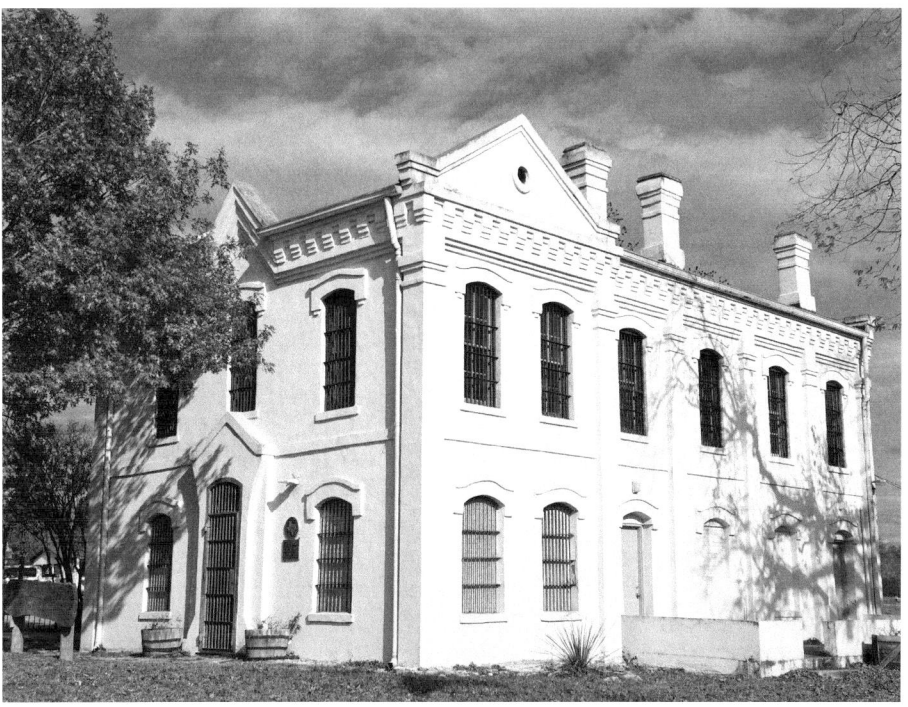

The two-story building was built in 1884. (*Darryl Pearson*)

## Beaumont Jail

The first county building constructed at this site was the jail, completed in 1838. John Beaumont built the first courthouse in 1854. By 1893, the population had grown, and the city needed a new courthouse.

In 1931, the city spent millions constructing the Jefferson County Courthouse and jail in Beaumont, Texas. The Art Deco-styled courthouse is fourteen stories high and one of the tallest in the state. It is also one of the earliest examples of Art Deco in Texas. The dedication day was January 17, 1932. The top five floors housed the jail from 1932 until 1981. The originality of the building has not changed since 1932. Located just one block from the Port of Beaumont, locals called the jail "Bar Harbor."

The advertised description of the new jail sounded nice. "Every conceivable convenience has been provided."

They provided electric refrigeration in the kitchen, ice water in each room, plenty of windows for sunlight, and steam heat in winter. The ad went on to detail the luxuries at "Bar Harbor" as if the city were renting out apartments: "Persons interested in taking an apartment in Bar Harbor are advised to contact the custodian, W.W. Covington, at the sheriff's office."

In 1905, smallpox spread through the jail.

In March 1922, Overnae Theriot committed suicide in his cell at Beaumont Jail by slashing his throat. He was found dead in his cell in the early morning.

In July 1923, a man named Newt DeSilva returned to Beaumont Jail. He had killed two men and received the death sentence but escaped the jail and fled to Mexico. While on the run, he killed two more men. Just after crossing the border back into Laredo, the sheriff of Webb County apprehended DeSilva and returned to his cell at Beaumont.

In June 1930, mobs threatened the jail. Officials arrested Rainey Williams, an African American man suspected of assaulting several white women. Five men calmly approached the sheriff early in the evening, demanding he free Williams. The sheriff remained firm and stated that the men needed to let the law take its course. By midnight, a crowd of over 200 gathered around the jail. By this point, both deputies and the mob held rifles. Deputies felt confident there was no possibility of anyone entering Williams' cell. The following day, the crowd remained. They refused to leave despite being ordered repeatedly.

As the inmates moved to the new facilities, visitors to the top floors began to hear the metallic clank of cell doors and strange moaning noises from the empty area.

Jefferson County is known as a hot spot for paranormal activity. During the era of lynching, only fifteen of the recorded 322 did not occur in East Texas. Jefferson

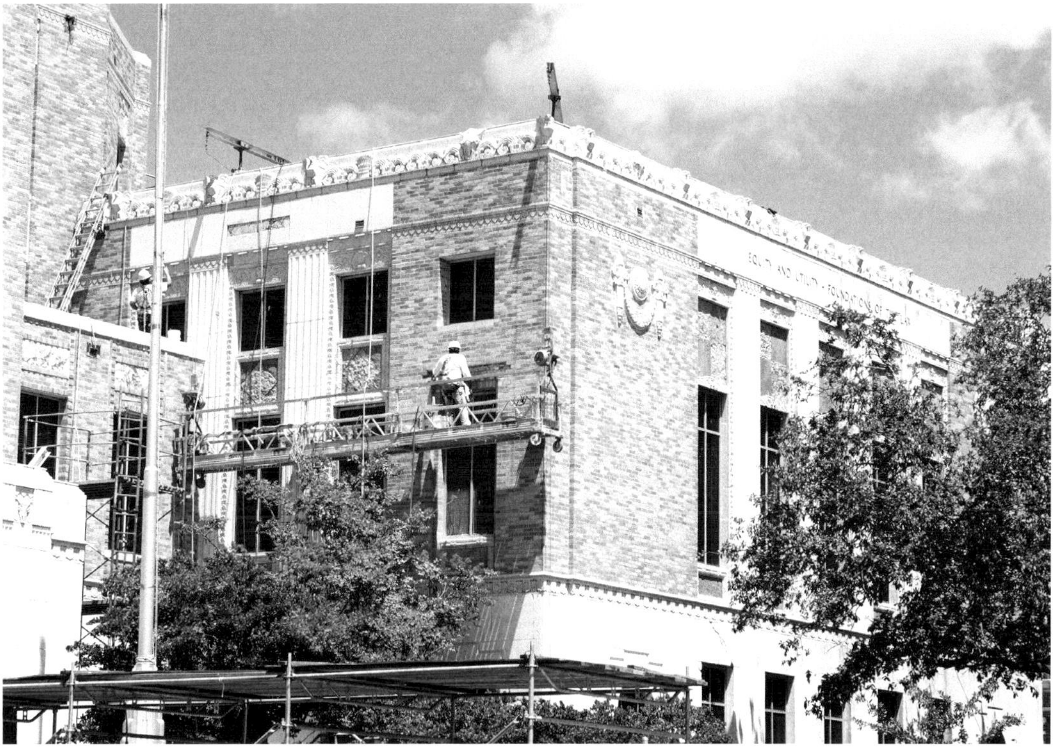

Renovations have been completed on the courthouse. (*Library of Congress*)

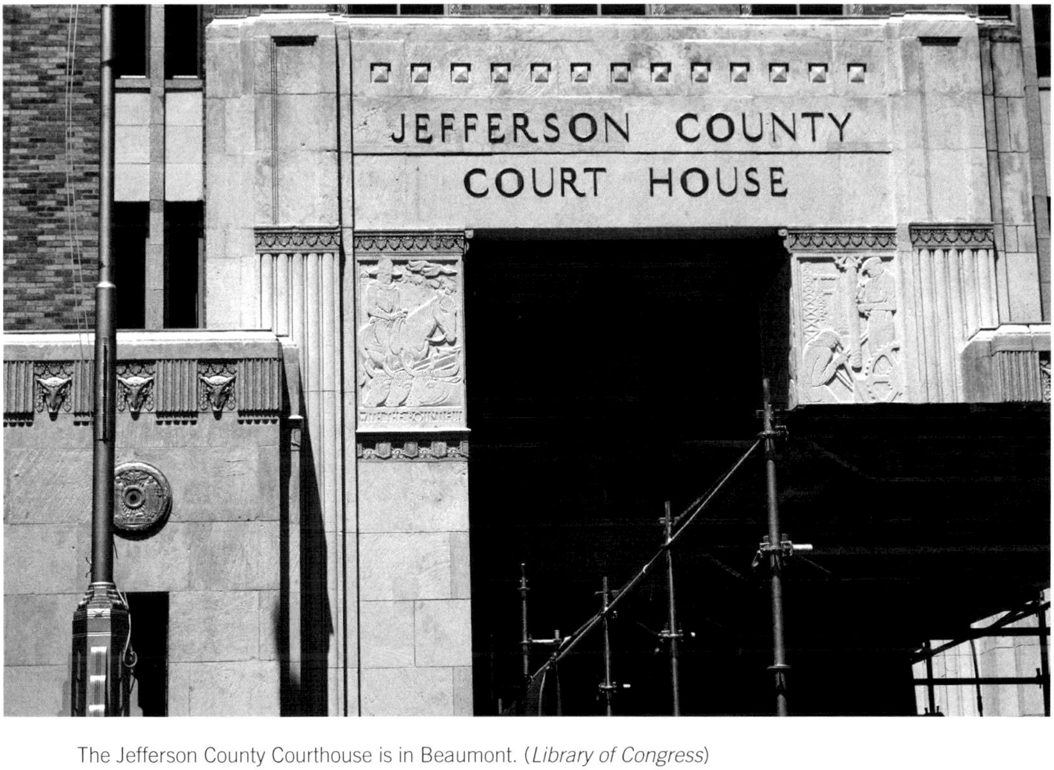

The Jefferson County Courthouse is in Beaumont. (*Library of Congress*)

served as an important trade center. It was the sixth-largest settlement. Rebel resentment and white supremacy formed a toxic brew in the early years of Jefferson.

A former union lieutenant, George Smith, advocated for the rights of formerly enslaved people. Black citizens elected him primarily to act as a delegate to the state constitutional convention. However, opponents stopped Smith short of his elected duties.

On October 3, 1868, Smith walked peacefully home from a Republican meeting with a friend. A group of townspeople approached the duo. A man Smith had argued with earlier in the day, Richard Crump, fired a shot aimed at Smith. Smith returned fire, hitting two men. They charged Smith with assault. He attempted to fight for sanctuary at a federal jail, but officials assured him he would be safe at the local jail. Four black men accompanied Smith. The following day, over seventy citizens met for the first incarnation of the Ku Klux Klan. Smith was shot and killed in his cell.

In the months following Smith's death, bands of armed terrorists came at night, burning homes and crops and bullying black citizens. The military declared martial law and began making arrests. Eventually, the tension settled down, and life became routine for the majority, but it left a haunted past for the entire city.

In 1981, the Beaumont Jail reached an official closed and abandoned status. Today boxes fill the empty rooms, which act as an area for surplus storage for the courthouse.

## Gonzales County Jail

The Gonzales County jail is a three-story building constructed of tan brick with a flat roof. In 1887 this new building replaced the first jail. A two-story space is in the interior of the northeast arm where the gallows stood. A hole in the ceiling reminds visitors of the area where the noose dropped, but officials removed the gallows in 1951. The building contained freestanding cell blocks on the second and third levels. Segregation happened according to gender and the severity of their crimes. The first floor housed the sheriff and jailers. At the end of a dark hallway lay the dungeon area, where only a peak of light entered the room. In the dungeon, inmates endured being restrained for hours and had no concept of night or day. The jail lacked heating, cooling, and sanitary facilities, preventing long-term lock-up. The jail primarily served as a temporary place to keep inmates before transferring to another location.

Copious executions took place in the gallows before all executions moved to Huntsville. Those inmates on death row had little to view except the gallows down the hallway.

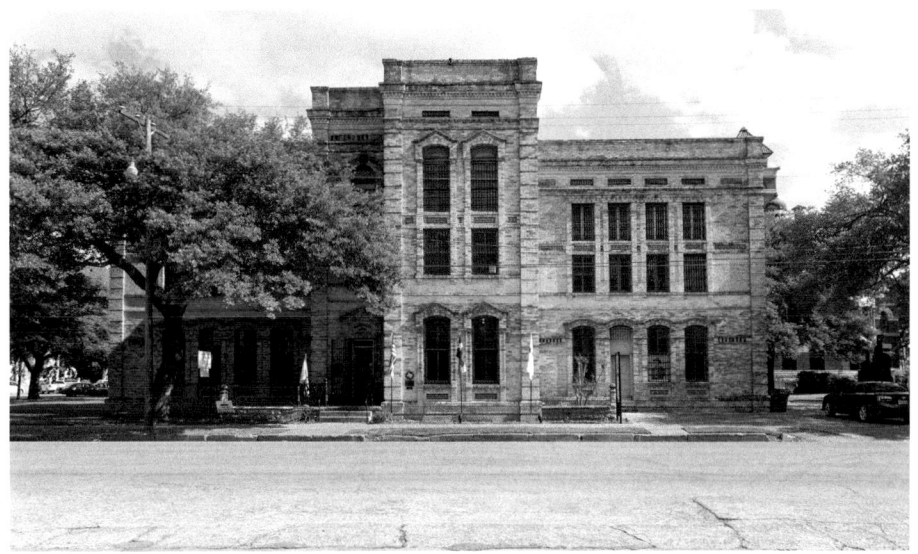

The jail was built in 1885 and closed in 1975. (*Carol Highsmith*)

In 1898, Jim Barber faced the gallows at Gonzales County Jail for the deliberate murder of his wife, Patsy. Barber and his wife lived in the servant house of Ed Scheske. The couple had been married for around five years. Barber worked as a successful butcher and a good businessman. Patsy tended to keep busy associating with male companions, which threw Barber into a jealous fit. The couple even separated for a short trial apart. On the night of her death, Patsy prepared to attend a dance. Her husband attempted to stop her, but she refused his pleas. Barber returned to the butcher shop where he worked and grabbed a pistol belonging to another employee. When he returned home, he passed several young girls playing on Scheske's lawn, and he found Patsy was dressed and ready for the dance. He entered the home, shut the door, and fired three shots from the borrowed pistol. Patsy's scream pierced the air, and the girls playing on the lawn ran to the windows to peer inside the tiny home. They met the evil sight of Barber performing butcher work on his wife. He shooed the girls away and returned to work without a second thought.

When officials entered the house, they found an iron barricade and Patsy's mangled body blocking the door. The bullet initially killed Patsy, but her blood and hair remained splattered across the room. Barber used a hatchet to chop away at her head and upper torso. He then used a knife to stab her until every ounce of life disappeared. Barber drew the blade across his throat, feebly attempting to take his own life. When questioned by police, Barber stated that Patsy initiated the attack by trying to cut his throat.

When brought before the court, the evidence was clear, and Barber received a death sentence by hanging at the gallows. The first legal hanging in the county occurred in 1856 when Frank Hill faced charges for the murder of A. D. Harris.

The county did not have another hanging until May 17, 1878, when a notorious outlaw named Brown Bowen murdered Thomas Haldeman. Bowen spotted Haldeman resting under a tree and walked up to the tree. Bowen shot Haldeman's brain out while he slept. Due to the notoriety of the inmate, the hanging was made public with over 5,000 in attendance. Officials built a scaffold outside of the jail.

In 1881, an African American named Isaiah Walker killed himself in a situation similar to Barber. Walker hung at the jail gallows.

In 1891, an African American named Will Blackwell was arrested and charged with murdering Lump Rainey. Since Blackwell's death, no other executions have occurred at this location.

In 1901, the jail held one of its most notorious inmates: a Mexican man named Gregorio Cortez. He became a folk hero in Mexico and the United States. Sheriff William "Brack" Morris came to the Thulemeyer Ranch to question Gregorio and Romaldo Cortez about a reported horse theft. Gregorio watched Romaldo as an altercation grew into a shootout. Romaldo charged the sheriff and was shot and wounded by Sheriff Morris. Gregorio opened fire and struck the sheriff four times. After Sheriff Morris fell to the ground, Cortez fired one last fatal shot. The story

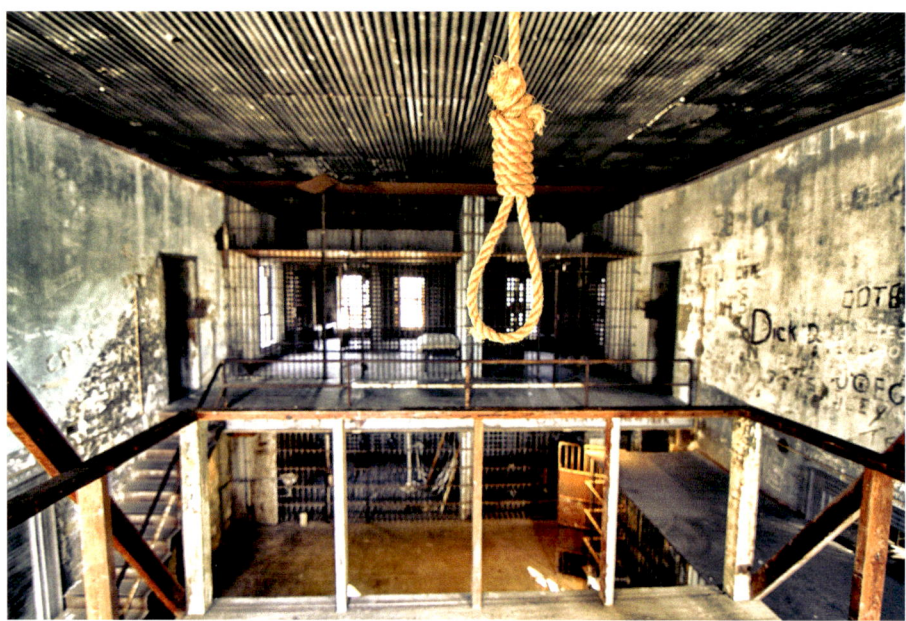

Makeshift gallows are accented with a hanging noose to offer guests an ominous feel. (Kelly Verdeck)

depends on who is telling it. Another version says Romaldo believed his brother was unarmed and ran into the sheriff to protect Gregorio. In this version, Gregorio shot at the sheriff in self-defense.

Just two days later, Cortez shot and killed Gonzales County Sheriff Richard Glover and one of his deputies, Henry Schnabel, when the men tried to arrest Cortez for the murder of Sheriff Morris. Sheriff Glover discovered where Gregorio was hiding and planned to ambush. The sheriff and his posse fired shots at the house. Gregorio fired back and killed the sheriff and one of his men. The Texas Rangers began a thirteen-day manhunt to bring in the man who killed two sheriffs. The Rangers captured Cortez on June 22, 1901. Authorities took him to the Gonzales County Jail for detainment. While some only saw him as a Mexican criminal, others saw a simple Mexican cowboy and dynamic leader of a well-organized band of thieves. Others felt he was a heroic figure who could outrun the mighty Texas Rangers.

Officials discovered Gregorio had traded a horse, and the error fell with a language barrier in which the misunderstanding came from deciding if it was a mare or stallion. The trial was extensive, but in the end, the jury found Gregorio Cortez guilty of second-degree murder and sentenced them to serve fifty years in prison. The verdict enraged many locals who expected the man sentenced to death for killing the lawmen. Just a few months after his conviction, a mob of over three hundred gathered to arrange a lynching. However, their attempt failed.

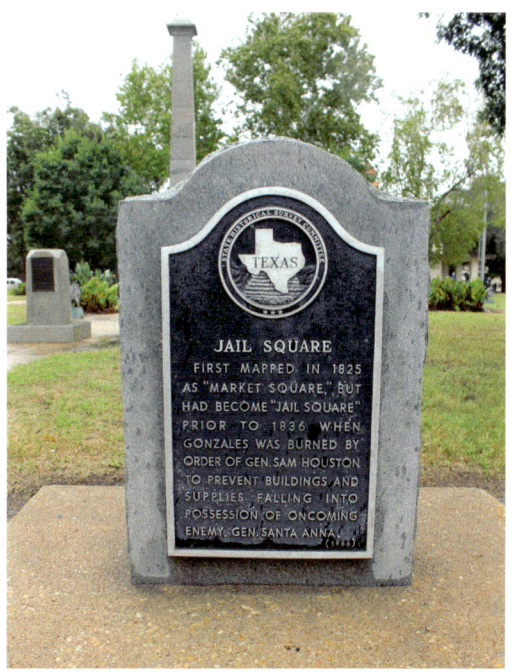

Bandits, outlaws, and bad guys have been housed at this jail. (*Nicholas Henderson*)

In January 1902, the Texas Court of Criminal Appeals reversed his sentence. They did not feel that Cortez could have killed both sheriffs in such a short time. After several appeals and months, no one could agree on how much time Cortez should serve and for what crimes. Eventually, he was cleared of the murder of Sheriff Morris, as the court believed he acted in self-defense. He was found guilty of murder by Sheriff Glover, and for this charge, on January 1, 1905, he began his life sentence at the Huntsville State Penitentiary.

In July 1913, Governor Oscar Colquitt issued a conditional pardon, and Gregorio Cortez was free. He went on to fight in the Mexican Revolution and remarried, but at age forty, he suddenly died. The cause of his death left people wondering if it was natural causes or if one of his enemies planted poison. His legend lives on in the Hollywood adaptation of his folklore: *The Ballad of Gregorio Cortez*.

Sandra Wolf gave Joe Perez of *Texas Chronicles* a tour of the old jail. She stated she feels the location has ghosts as many people have entered but ran out and never returned to the area. She recounted the story of a seventeen-year-old male who toured the jail with his mother. He had stepped away from his mom and traveled to the cell at the end of the last row. The cell belonged to the notorious Gregorio Cortez. He noted a handprint on the wall and placed his hand on the print. At the same time, he felt as if someone had approached from behind. He turned to see a man in a blue shirt with a shaggy beard and hair. The young man quickly left the cell and went down the hallway. When he stopped to glance into a different cell, he spotted the same man sitting on a cot. He promptly found his mother and left the museum. He has not returned.

A total of six inmates died via the gallows at the Gonzales County Jail between 1855 and 1921. Four are said to have occurred outside the jail, and two within the walls. The final man to die via the gallows was a man by the name of Albert Howard. Howard was nineteen when arrested on rape and robbery charges. He declared his innocence from the point of his arrest. He agreed he was present when the crime occurred and witnessed the crime but did not take part. From his cell, Howard could view two sides of the clock tower outside. As the jailers brought him to the gallows, he pleaded for release.

He stated, "If I am an innocent man, the clock faces on the tower will never match with the same time after my death."

Instead, Howard's innocence or guilt is still unclear, but the faces on the clock tower begin to function ominously. They didn't read simultaneously, no matter the effort. In the 1990s, the original parts of the clock retired. With new components, the clock began to sync with time on each face of the tower.

Investigative teams have entered the old jail to determine if they can discover paranormal activity. Investigators from the YouTube channel *Strange Chronicles from*

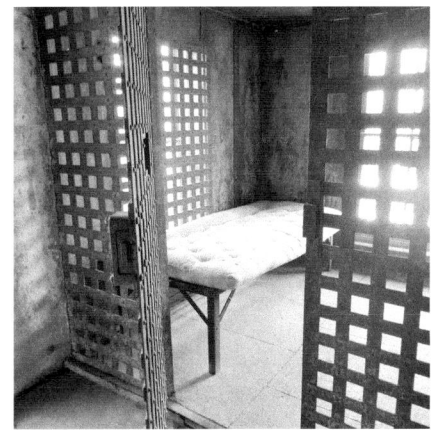

Three executions took place at this location before 1924. (*National Historic Register*)

*the Graveyard Shift* explored the abandoned prison in August 2014. They heard and recorded footsteps and a camera continually going in and out of focus. The collected electronic voice phenomena, or EVPs, sounded much like the following:

"Hurt me."

"Grab her." Investigators heard this as a female investigator passed.

"Felon."

The abandoned jail is a museum; tourists can walk through the cells and view a replica of the original gallows. The museum displays items in cases that tell about law enforcement officers who served there over the years and contraband confiscated from prisoners. Visitors to the museum report having their hair pulled and scratches appearing on their bodies. They heard footsteps and whistling. They also saw shadows from the corner of their eye and experience nausea. Perhaps the inmates remained in their cells and never left the jail.

## IMPERIAL PRISON FARM

Before the Civil War, Sugarland, Texas, was known for its cotton, corn, and sugar cane crops. The small town thrived on sugar production, and the Imperial Sugar Company provided employment.

In 1865, emancipated indentured servants and plantation owners struggled to find field workers. In 1878, two landowners negotiated with the State of Texas to lease their land for a private prison that would house convicts to provide labor for the fields. This practice was common in the South during the Reconstruction period. The state could generate profitable revenue, and plantations receive laborers. During a time when some could not afford to pay the penalty for their crime via cash, they could exchange this by working off their debt to the state. Of course, monitoring did not occur. The state made good money, so it was common to see charges on those they knew could not pay.

In 1908, the State of Texas bought 5,235 acres of land and began constructing the Imperial State Prison Farm on the Imperial Sugar Plantation. The prison was one of the first state-operated prisons in Texas and housed about 400 inmates. It was known at the start to apply deplorable living conditions and treatment of the inmates.

In 1930, the prison underwent a name change to be called the Central State Prison. The name originated from the prison, the agricultural goods' central farming and distribution center. The state approved funding for constructing a new unit to Central Farm and completed the build in late 1932. The state planned Central to become the correctional system's central intake and rehabilitation prison.

In 1935, the prison housed black and white prisoners but segregated them by race. By 1950, the prison held over 1,000 prisoners. In 1991, the prison gave land to the transportation department to develop roads; by 2007, the prison only had 336 acres.

In March 2007, a prisoner escaped the Central Prison. Thirty-nine-year-old David Roberts managed to escape just before the headcount. Roberts was in the trustee program due to his excellent behavior, and in less than two years, he would be eligible for parole. Officials found him hiding at his mom's house.

In 2007, talks of closure began, but in 2011, Texas legislators voted to close the prison by removing funding. The only hesitation was how to move 1,500 prisoners and where to move them. Within one month, the prison closed after 112 years of operation.

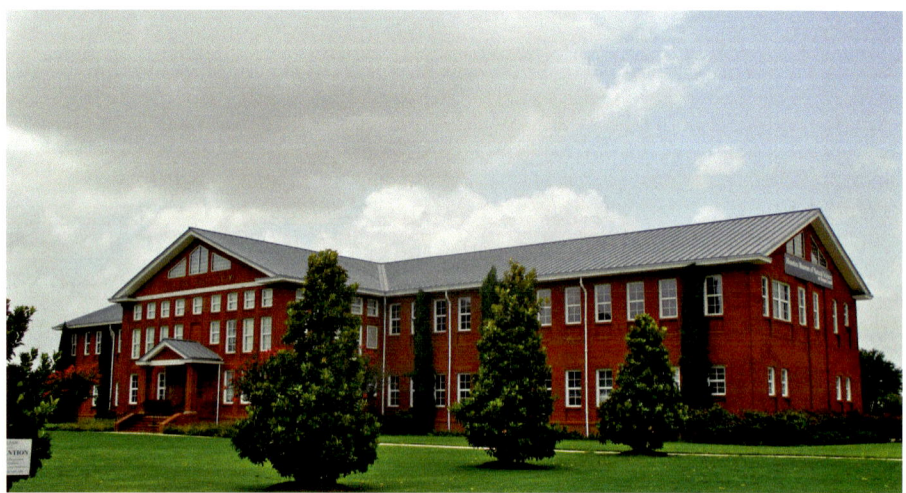

The prison had a farm that helped to provide work to keep inmates busy and food for them to eat. (*Robert Perkins*)

The Imperial Prison Cemetery holds thirty-one marked graves of inmates and guards and at least two unmarked graves. Some of the tombstones contain graphic descriptions of the case of death, and in the center of the cemetery, prisoners constructed a sizeable white cross surrounded by red bricks in the shape of a star.

Ghost and horror stories linger in the not-so-sweet Sugarland prison. Researchers started working to identify almost one hundred young men who were former convicts buried near the prison. Most of these individuals are considered African Americans who fell victim to the convict leasing program. Society forgot these souls and left them in an abandoned cemetery. Most felt convict leasing was "slavery by another name" as it targeted black men with questionable charges and harsh sentences. Historians agree that the conditions were cruel. When the Fort Bend School District began clearing land, they knew they could find bones and burials. Researchers continued identifying the bodies and painstakingly moved them to another location for proper honor and burial. The Fort Bend School District plans to honor the forgotten soul with a memorial, but ghosts may still haunt the new school.

In 1892, sixteen-year-old William Nash received a sentence of four years in prison for property theft. However, his remains are at the prison cemetery. His cause of death stemmed from traumatic brain injury obtained while working under treacherous conditions. His body lay among the dishonored, but he can finally rest peacefully.

The Central Unit gained fame by appearing on *Ghost Adventures* on September 14, 2012. The prison closed one year before the investigation. The investigative crew went in as a blind investigation, which means they had little to no information

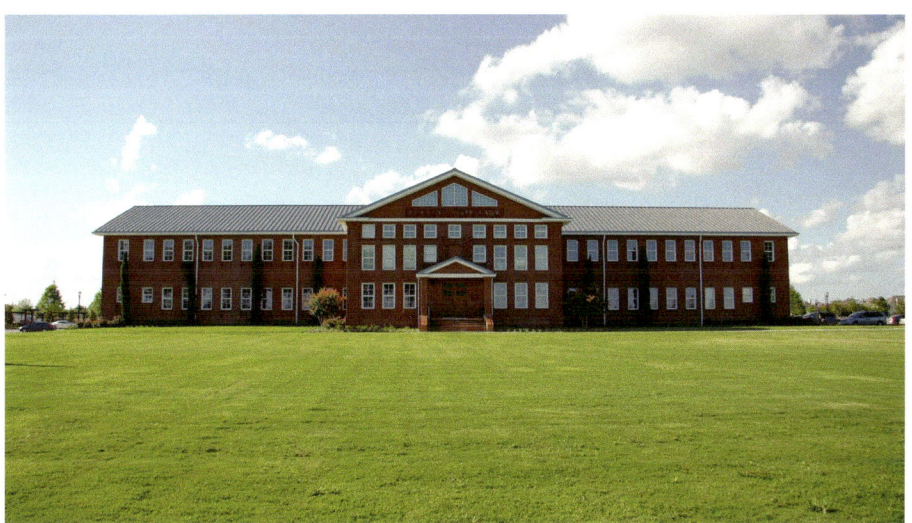

The prison first opened in 1909 and did not close until 2011. (*Robert Perkins*)

about the location. Blind investigations are a preferred method as they can help validate findings.

Bruce Kelly, a historian, offered some historical background to the location. The investigators spoke to a father of a former inmate who witnessed riots, fights, and suicide in the solitary confinement area. A former guard told the team he felt a hand resting on his shoulder.

One of the investigators captured a figure standing near some equipment cases he was photographing utilizing a full spectrum camera that picks up temperature variations. As the team leader, Zak Bagans decided to investigate where the suicide occurred. Bagans noted a spike on his Mel Meter, a ghost-hunting device that detects electromagnetic fields and temperature. One of the cameras began to go in and out of focus. During the review of the evidence, the team found a voice spirit box, and they captured an EVP (electronic voice phenomenon).

By this point in the investigation of the men, Nick Groff began to feel fatigued, shaken, and emotional. The team stepped outside to re-group. Several unexplainable bangs occured throughout the night. Just before the crew left, they received one last message from the inmates at Central Unit: "Goodbye."

Through the investigation, they noted that the unexplained bangs occurred around five times. Groff states he felt a push by an unseen force and then felt like he was not himself. They saw a black, shadow figure move across a door. They caught a figure on the thermal imaging camera. They experienced troubles with their cameras and equipment, which can symbolize spirits attempting to use electricity to present themselves.

Is the Ghost Hunters' investigation proof of ghosts in lockdown? It is possible, but no other investigators have been allowed inside the facility, and the evidence they collected shows proof of paranormal activity.

## Old Williamson County Jail

Williamson County's third jail resided on the east lawn of the courthouse and was a freestanding building. Only two jail cells meant overcrowding existed. The penitentiary closed in October 1888, and prisoners moved to Travis County until the new prison reached completion. Too many escapes occurred to risk leaving the inmates at the Williamson County Jail. One day, six inmates escaped through a hole in the steel ceiling. Another flight happened a few weeks later. The men opened a corridor and dropped to the ground. Initially, people believed the jail was in good condition and that repairing the structure was the best solution.

Funding for the new jail came from state bonds. These donated funds purchased the land from many of Williamson County's most prominent citizens. The doors for the new prison opened in January 1889, about four blocks north of the courthouse. An architectural firm from Waco drew up the plans for a two-story jail with three rooms and a hall on each floor. The stone prison had 18-inch-thick walls and bore stone cornices and stonework.

The only well-lit and ventilated enclosures were upstairs and housed women and the insane. These cells had access to water for washing, bathing, and drinking. The completed jail had ten cells which could each hold four people. This jail remained open until 1989.

Notorious serial killer Henry Lee Lucas spent time as an inmate at the jail. Lucas obtained his first murder charge in 1960 when he killed his mother. Lucas received two additional charges in 1983. He rose to fame after admitting to over six hundred murders during his killing spree. Law enforcement resolved several cold case files after the confessions. Ultimately, he was convicted of eleven murders and sentenced to death. Further investigations confirmed that Lucus lied about several of the murder confessions. The death sentence converted to life in prison, and he died of congestive heart failure in 2001.

Alma Reese was born in 1889 in Williamson County. On May 11, 1905, Tom Young viciously assaulted his stepdaughter. Young used a hoe, a chain, and a whip to assault and kill the young woman. He was a cotton harvester with a history of evil deeds. Young stole horses and was known as a bigamist.

On May 8, 1095, a group of farmers reported to the sheriff. Tom Young was beating his little girl. When two men arrived to check out the scene, Young ran. He had a knife, but the other men had six shooters. The men held Young until law enforcement came and delivered him to jail. His wife faced charges, but authorities agreed to release her in exchange for a detailed report on Young's abuse.

When Alma was one, Young promised her mother that he and his wife would provide a good home for the child. As she aged and began to travel into town more with her stepfather, people noted something was off with the family. Alma was in poor condition, and when questioned by townspeople, she confessed to Young's abuse.

When the medical examiner reviewed her body at the morgue, he proved that many of the stories were true. Parts of Alma's scalp showed abrasions. One of her wounds held gangrene which had moved into her bones. Evidence also pointed to brutal sexual abuse.

Mrs. Young testified, "Tom whipped her for three hours while she was chained to a post and with blood running down her body. She cried out, 'O kill me now. I can't stand this.' As he threw acid in her wounds."

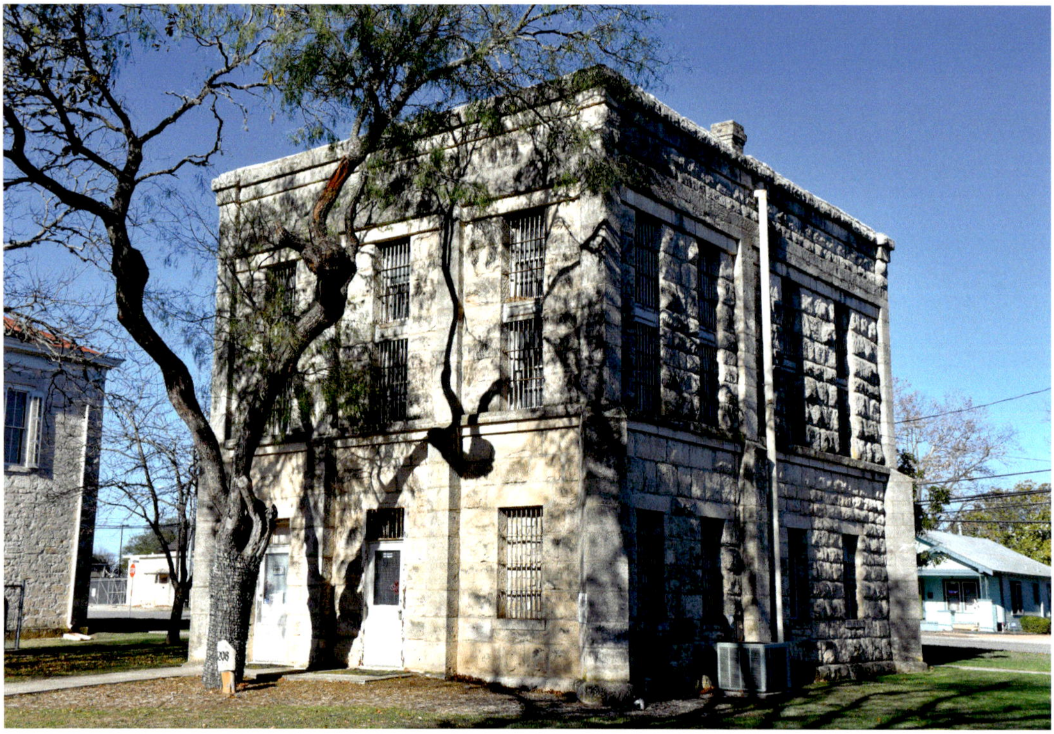

The jail was located on the east lawn of the courthouse. (*Craig Hanchey*)

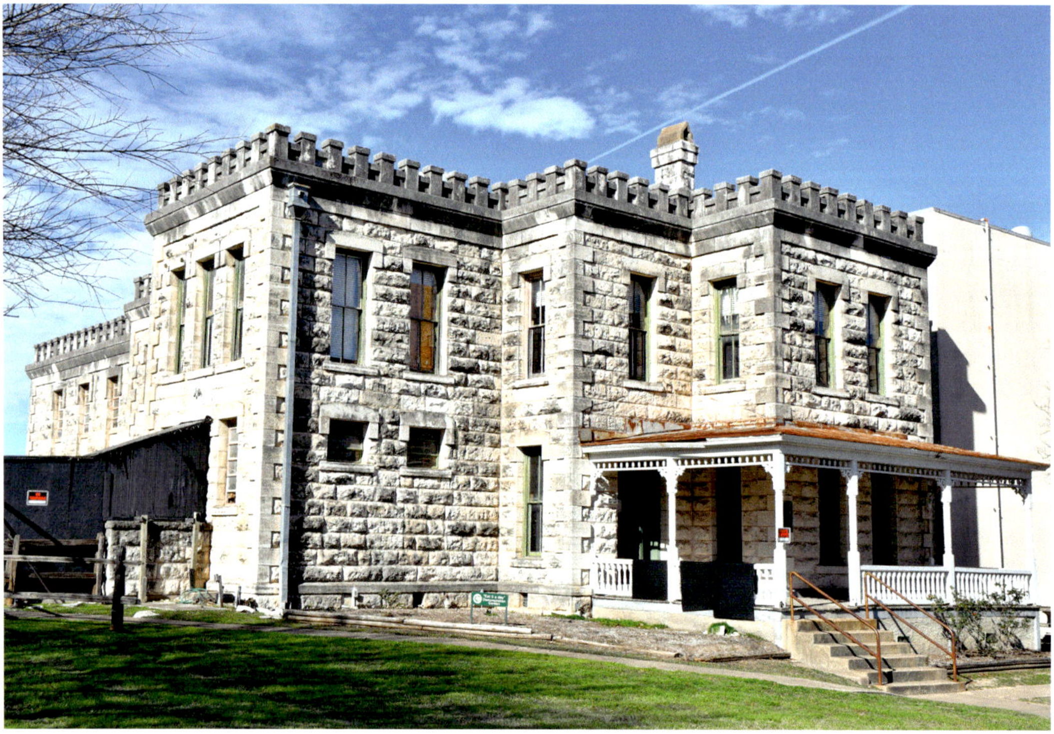

It opened its doors in 1888. (*Craig Hanchey*)

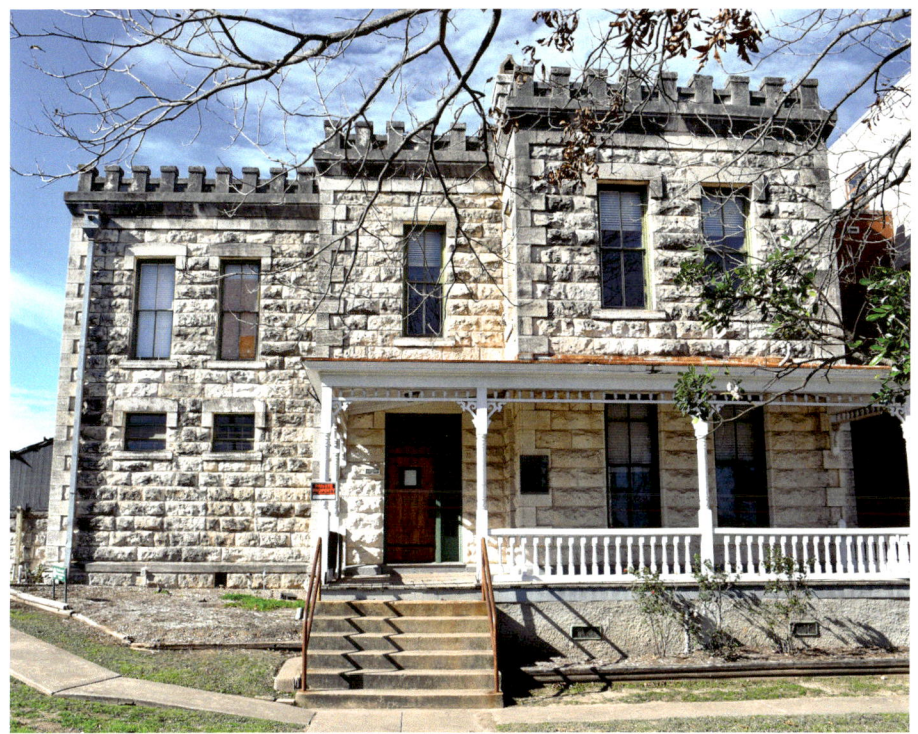

Prisoners were moved to a larger facility due to the number of escapees. (*Craig Hanchey*)

At the end of the trial, the verdict was clear. Tom Young was charged with the brutal murder of Alma Reese and hung until his death. The courtroom buzzed with whistles and cheers.

Young was escorted to the gallows in Georgetown to an open field at the poor farm. After forgetting the black cap for his head and a man asking Young questions, the hanging proceeded. Young was the last man executed in Williamson County.

In 1933, Louis Cernoch used abusive language on a woman. Constable Sam Moore brought Cernoch before the judge. The judge ruled that Cernoch was to pay a small fine and had thirty days to comply. When he had not paid his penalty, Constable Moore went to the farm where Cernoch worked to make an arrest. Cernoch asked to go back into the farmhouse to change clothes. Constable Moore failed to search Cernoch, which would be a fatal error. When taken to the judge's office, Cernoch pulled out a pistol and fired on Constable Moore and City Marshal Henry Lindsay. Lindsay died instantly, and Moore succumbed to his injuries a few hours later. The judge took refuge behind office furniture as shots aimed at him went wild across the room. He received only a scratch as a bullet grazed his leg. Cernoch was tackled and taken into custody. Now he faced two murder charges and one attempted murder charge. He was held at Williamson County Jail and sentenced to death. He died in the electric chair in Huntsville just ninety days later.

Another man, Pedro Cruz Muniz, faced arrest. Janis Bickham was only nineteen when she was kidnapped, raped, and murdered on December 20, 1976, by Muniz. He admitted to his crimes and received a lethal injection in 1998.

The jail held its last prisoner in 1989. It is easy to see that the jail bars have held back a menagerie of dark characters over the years.

The stone exterior dominates and could show visitors what is in store and dark, spooky energies. Workers claim they have items tossed off shelves and desks. Cold spots, disembodied voices, and footsteps occur daily. Nearly all visitors report an uneasy feeling of being watched. A Williamson County law officer said, "Strange things happen here."

The officer reports witnessing paranormal activity during formal investigations at the old jail. At one point, he heard a voice in the hallway calling his name. He was the only one inside the building.

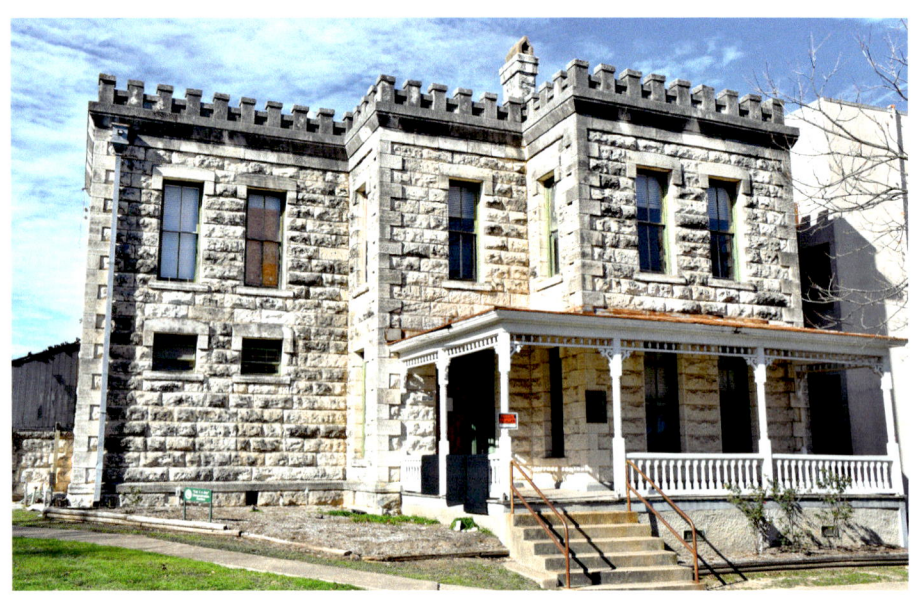

Many believe the jail is haunted by the bad guys who spent their time behind bars and could not escape. (*Craig Hanchey*)

# 3

# PAGING DR. CASPER

## Bexar County Juvenile Home for Boys

During the nineteenth century, poorhouses offered a stable living arrangement for indigent people. Poorhouses offered non-disabled citizens a way to work and live in a safe environment. They were set up as farms to provide milk, eggs, fruits, and vegetables to those working on the farm. Often, the elderly and disabled found themselves at the poorhouses and supported by the state or the county. Due to the ill health of many residents, inevitable deaths occurred at this location, which was built in 1915. Shortly after, an additional building was added to the farm and housed the Bexar County Juvenile Home for Boys. Many believe these deaths and tragedies helped to create the ghost stories associated with the structure.

The juvenile home for boys had a few mishaps over its existence. Whenever one gathers a group of rebellious youths, trouble blossoms.

On January 26, 1925, officials located a fourteen-year-old inmate named Alfred Garcia, semiconscious. The attendant called for assistance, and Garcia went to the local hospital. He survived. Doctors discovered he had ingested rat poison but could not determine if it was foul play or pure accident.

The facility made headlines again in November 1933 when a thirteen-year-old inmate named Charles Watson was killed. According to his death certificate, Watson's murder occurred on November 2, 1933, and his body was located in a creek over 1 mile away thirteen days later. His cause of death lists a skull fracture with an iron prison pipe. Jesus Samudio, a twenty-one-year-old farmhand at the facility, was accused and tried for Watson's murder. Samudio confessed, giving a complete, detailed account of the murder. He claimed the two fought over cleaning milk bottles.

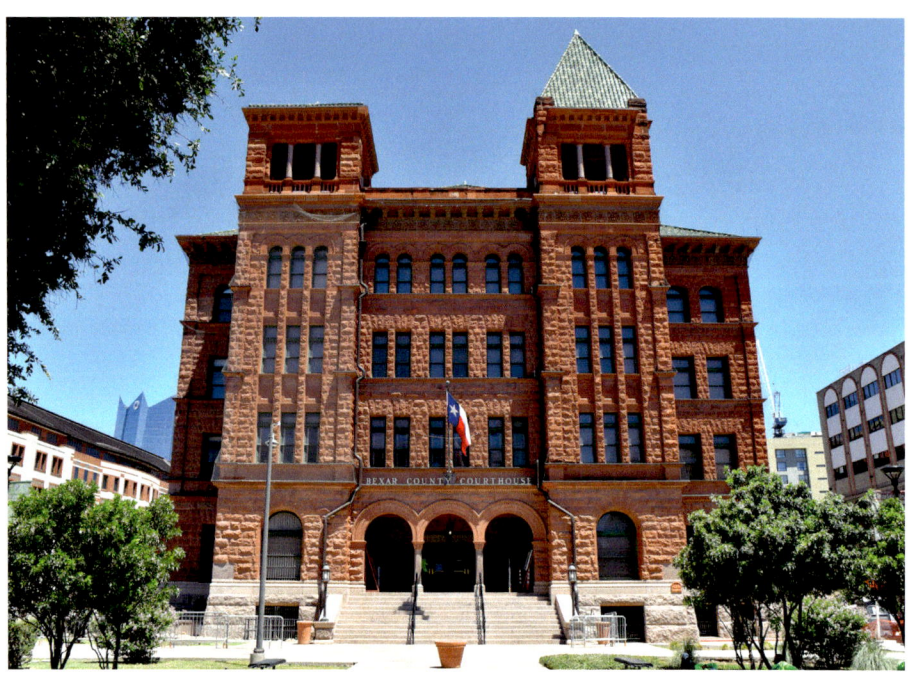
Then Bexar County Courthouse may have been the first stop for many of the boys at Bexar. (*Craig Hanchey*)

Sometime around 1960, the poorhouse functioned as a nursing home. By 1968, they relocated the boys to a new detention center, and the nursing home residents moved out in 1969, leaving the property abandoned. In 1974, over 2,000 bodies needed to be excavated and moved. Some of the bodies belonged to residents of the poorhouse. Still, around 75 percent of the bodies belong to unidentified babies, with burials preceding building of the structures in 1915.

Few have explored this abandoned location as it is within visual distance of the new detention center and heavily guarded by police and perhaps a few angry ghosts. Those who have explored here tell stories about an abandoned site's mysterious nature. All four structures on the property are in ruins. There are reports of screams, moaning, doors slamming suddenly, creaking back open, and lots of footsteps.

One man stated he felt cold spots all over the building despite the Texas summer heat. Another woman described the same phenomenon; she also reported the large, heavy door slamming behind her after she entered the building, as if a detention center guard was securing the building. Another visitor came at night and reported she attempted to go to the top floor of the building but did not make it that far before she heard loud moaning and screaming. They dashed out of the building and vowed never to return.

Another male visitor states he heard a shotgun blast upon entering the building. However, this was most likely a neighbor firing a warning shot to scare them away. While exploring, he reports seeing a small female child wearing a white dress.

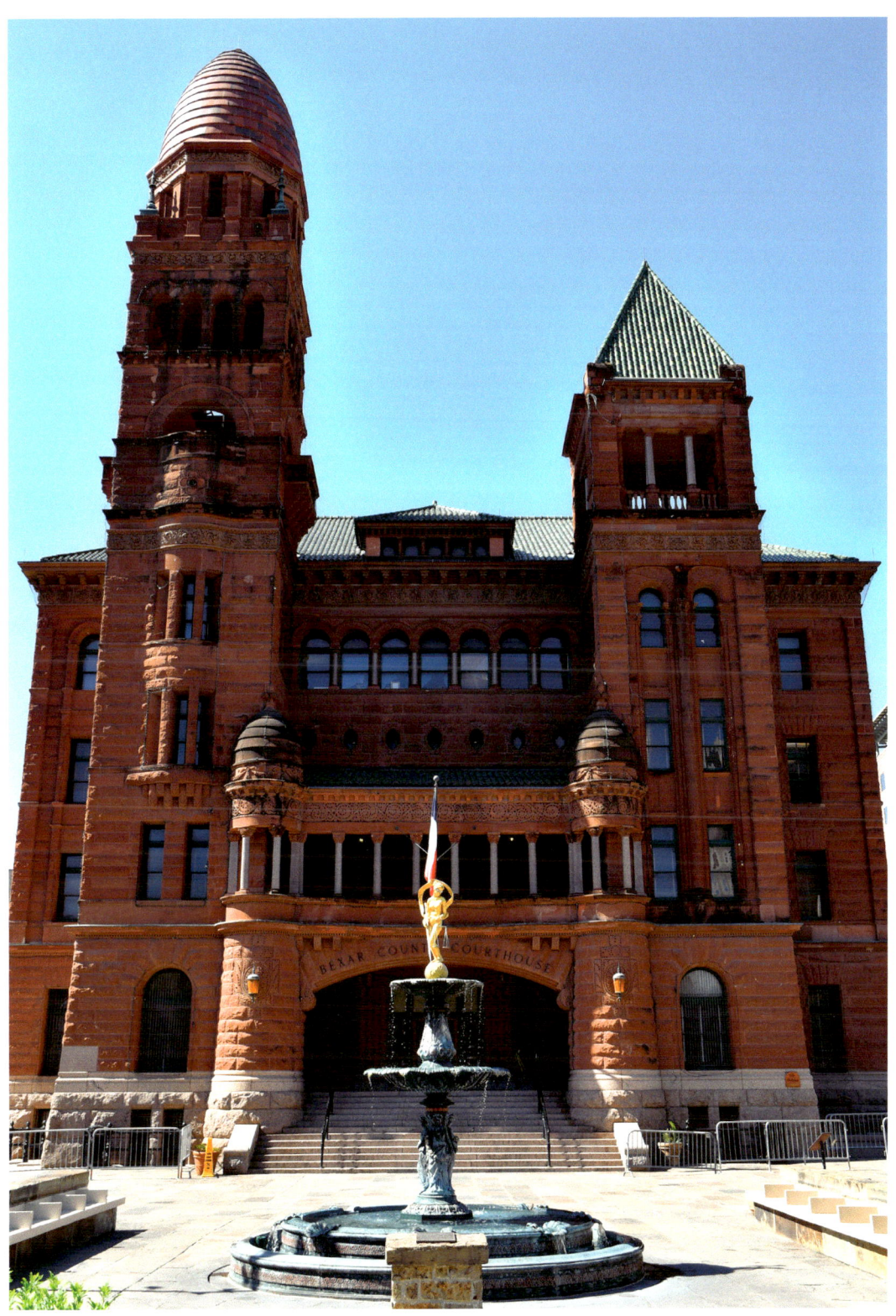
Vandals have greatly destroyed the building of the boys' home. (*Craig Hanchey*)

When he approached, she began to moan. He turned to go down a set of stairs and heard loud stomping as if from a heavy person. He turned only to see the girl in the white dress. He felt she might be protecting him from whoever made the loud stomps. He also claims he heard screaming and doors slamming. He too quickly exited and vowed never to return.

## Jefferson Davis Hospital

Always start at the base when researching the history of a location. This base begins in Houston, Texas. The finding could be surprising or even haunting. Before the construction of Jefferson Davis Hospital, the lot stood as a municipal burial ground. In the 1840s, the area needed to replace the Old City Cemetery, one of Houston's oldest sites. This new lot became the final resting place for over six thousand Confederate soldiers, forever enslaved people, and even city officials. Thousands of victims of yellow fever and cholera lay on the grounds too. The city discontinued using the grounds as a cemetery in 1879, but people continued to bury loved ones there until the 1890s. From there forward, the grounds were not maintained and began to deteriorate. The makeshift cemetery became abandoned.

When Houston began talks of building a hospital, more than a few concerned citizens spoke up about the possible disruption of the former residents who laid 6 feet under the soil. Due to the state of the graves, an alternate location was not an option for many of the burials. Most remained, and to prevent disruption, the hospital floor plans called from an above-ground basement. The basement meant a concrete foundation sealed in the remaining graves.

The hospital opened its doors in 1925 under the name Jefferson Davis Hospital to appease the Confederate soldiers' unrested spirits. Would these souls accept an entire hospital covering their graves simply because the name honored the president of the Confederacy?

The hospital stayed open for about thirteen years, but the Houston area was growing and thriving. The small building could not care for the population, so the hospital officially closed in 1939.

The building remained and served many different uses over the next fifty-one years. It was a community clinic, a mental asylum, and a psychiatric treatment center. It served as a storage area for medical records, a convalescing home, a venereal disease clinic, a home for juvenile delinquents, a drug treatment center, and even a food stamp distribution center.

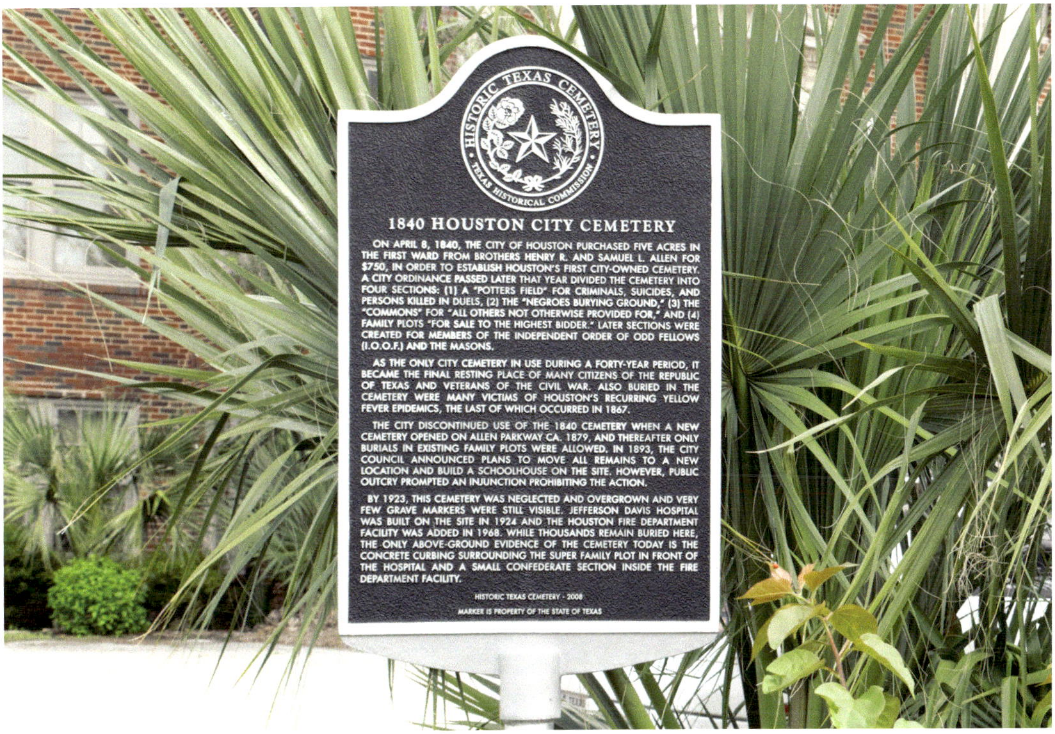

The lot was used as a cemetery before the hospital was built. (*Patrick Feller*)

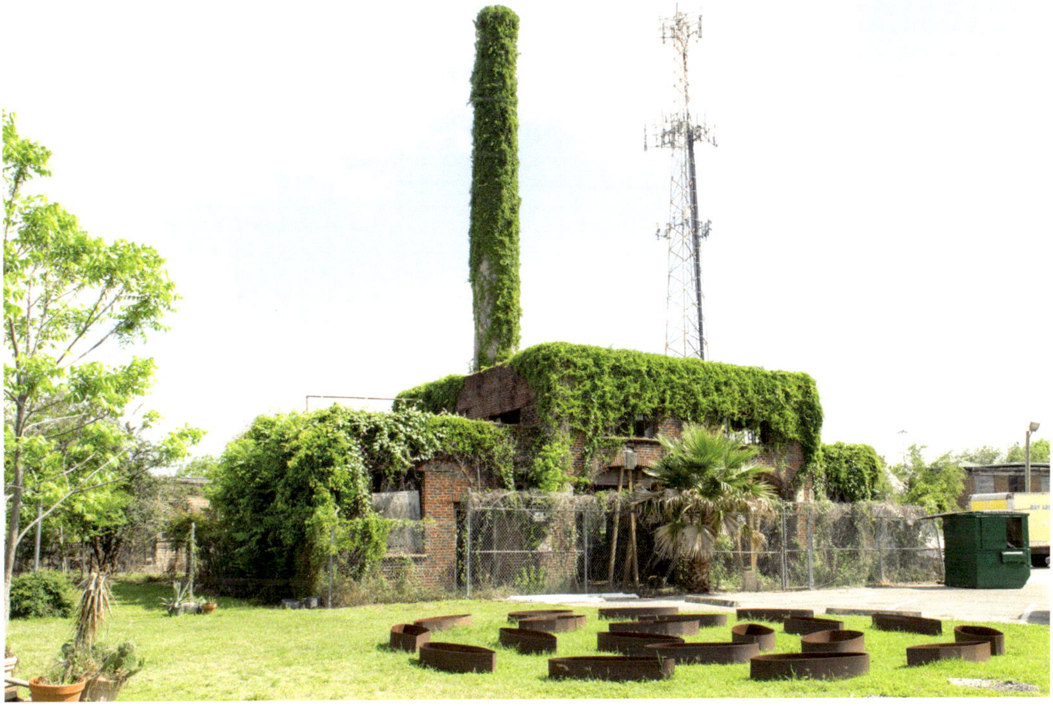

After years of neglect, the incinerator has been reclaimed by Mother Nature. (*Patrick Feller*)

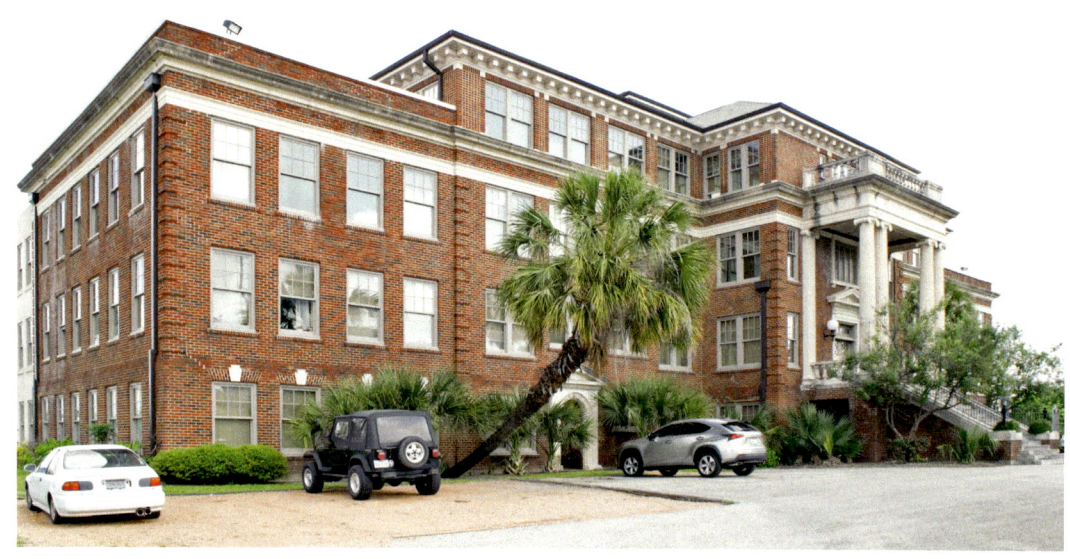

The red brick exterior resembles a resort hotel with large white pillars at the entrance. (*Patrick Feller*)

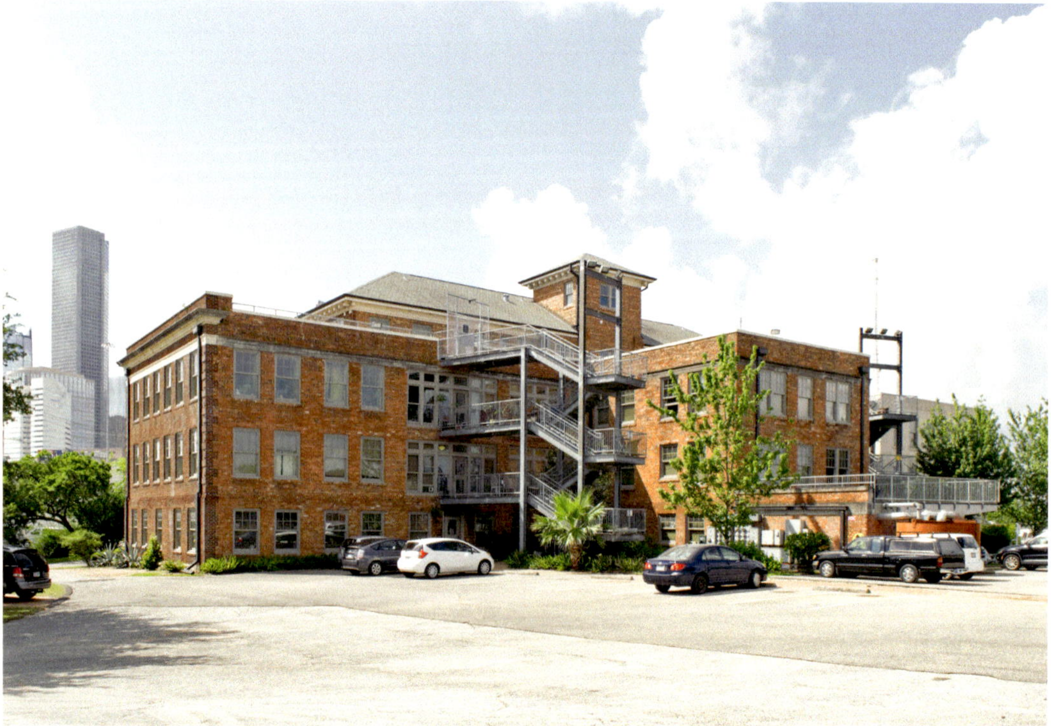

The hospital opened in 1924 and closed in 1939. (*Patrick Feller*)

The haunting stories started when the old building housed a probation office. The probation office extended to the building next door, which housed the former morgue. The two buildings covered the bodies of thousands of deceased.

Someone spotted a woman in the upper stories, which may have served as a dormitory for hospital nurses. Strange noises echo through the attic, and feminine figures float in and out of the bathrooms. Many times, the fire alarms sounded. Police and firefighters responded, but most, including their dogs, refused to enter the building at night.

In the late 1980s, the building became abandoned.

The City of Houston Archeological and Historical Commission saved the building in March 2002 when they approved a notion to declare it a city landmark. Rehabilitation of the building began in 2004, and today the building serves Elder Street Artist Lofts. Few abandoned locations reach the level of being refurbished or recycled. Some fear this was not the right option. Perhaps that is why it is known as one of the most haunted locations in South Texas. Visitors report shadow figures, the sensation of being watched, and the rich smell of hospital-grade sterilization products.

## Yorktown Memorial Hospital

What creates more fear: an old, abandoned hospital or an angry nun? What if a location featured both items? Traveling down the Old Indianola Trail brings visitors

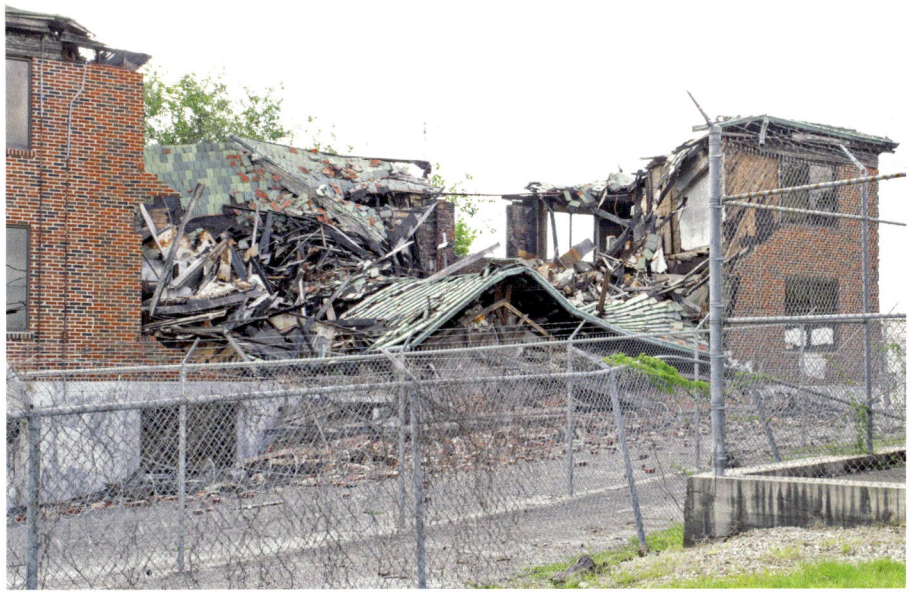

The hospital gained notoriety as one of the state's most haunted locations. (*Patrick Feller*)

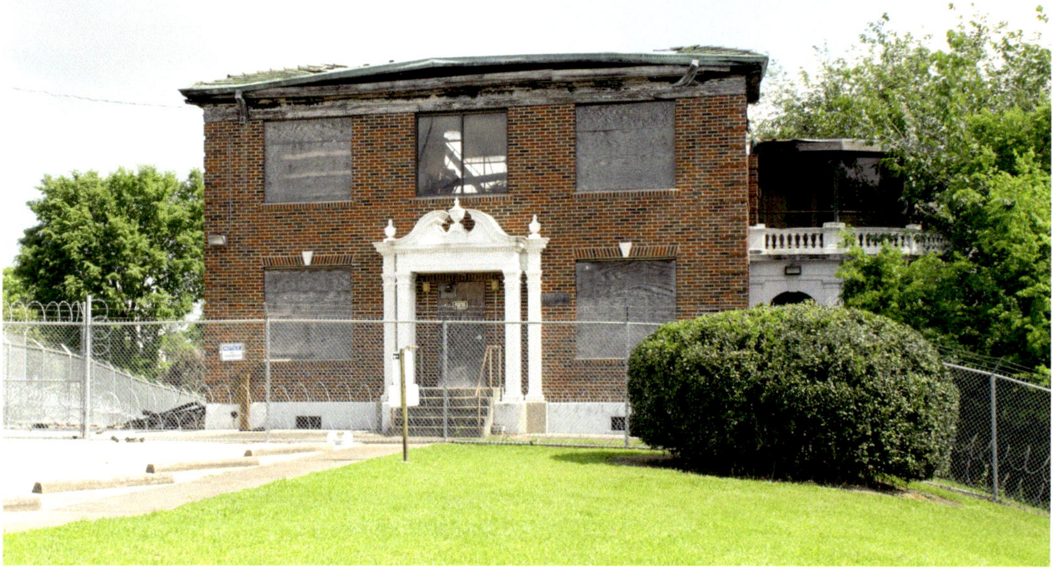

As construction was completed, the builders attempted to prevent disturbing the graves. (*Patrick Feller*)

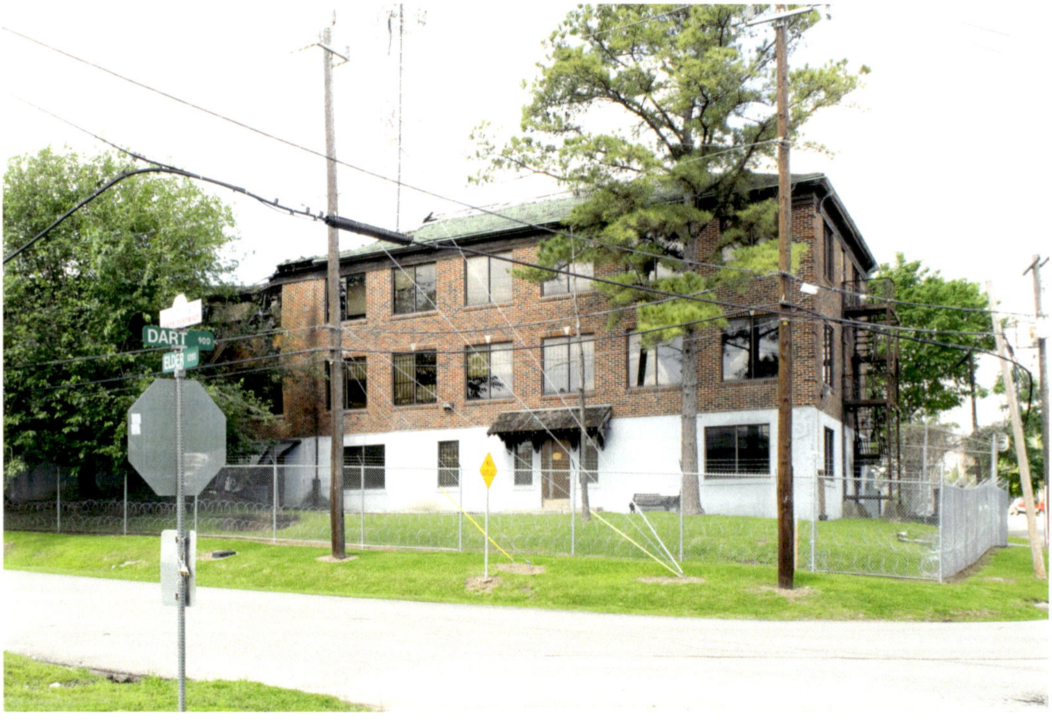

Named for the former president of the Confederacy, many Confederate soldiers were buried here. (*Patrick Feller*)

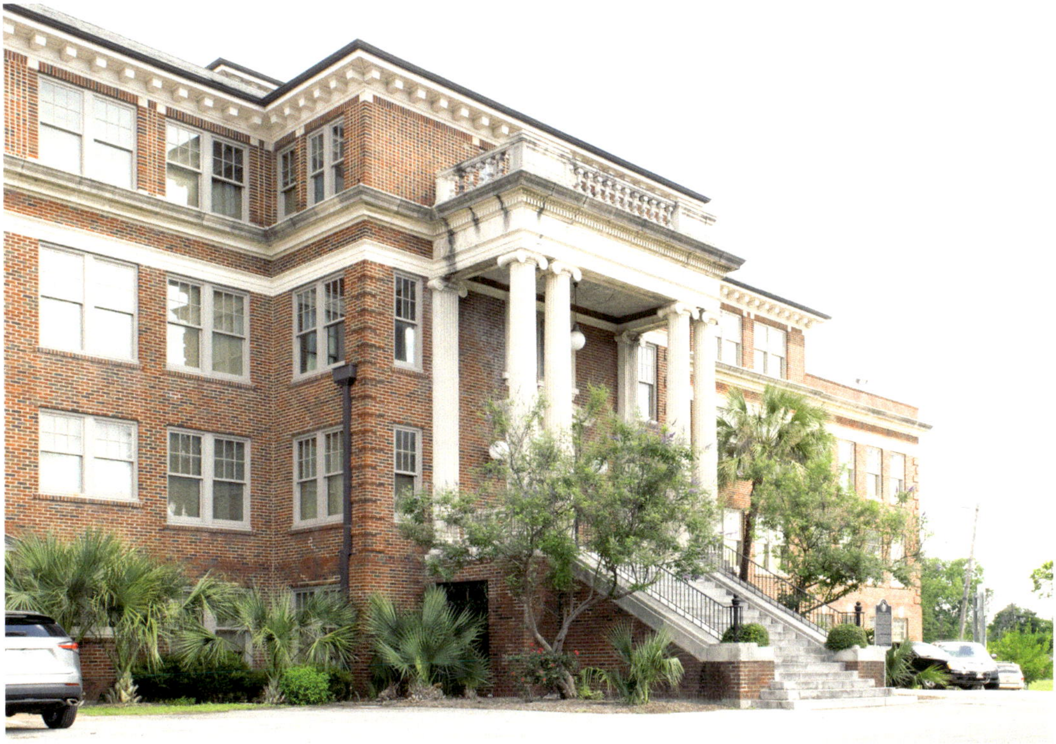

The fire alarm at the old hospital triggers itself at night. (*Patrick Feller*)

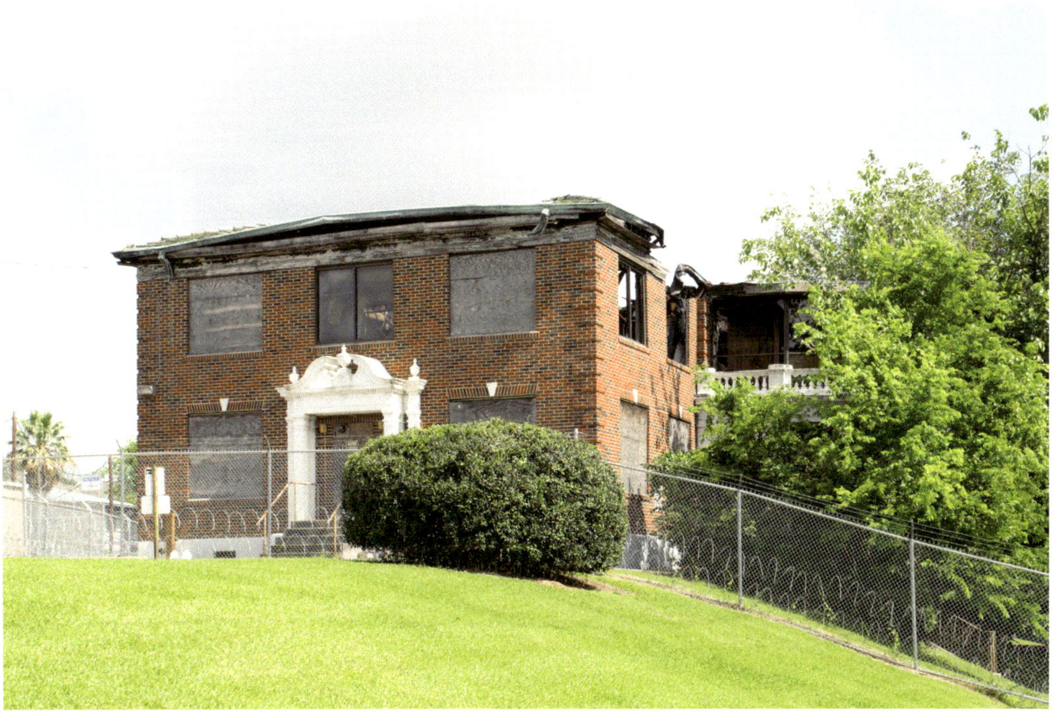

The site was officially abandoned in 1989 and began to fall into disrepair. (*Patrick Feller*)

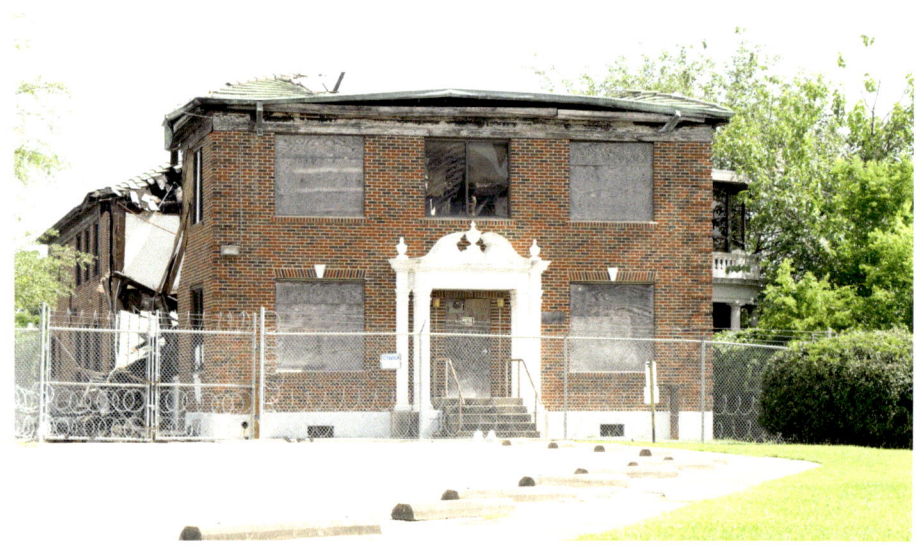

The restoration was completed in 2005, but part of the building remained closed. (*Patrick Feller*)

from the Gulf Coast to New Braunfels. In between those destinations sit Yorktown, Texas. Captain John York and Charles Eckhardt founded Yorktown in early 1848. York lost his life in a battle with Indigenous Americans who raided the Yorktown settlement in the fall of 1848. Eckhardt passed in 1852 before the Yorktown population increased.

The town grew despite the founders dying. Settlers knew the value of a stable education and erected a school in 1853 and a church four years later. The town became an essential stop for prairie schooners and trail drivers. It was incorporated in 1871 and grew steadily when the railroad came through town. By 1898, the city thrived with over sixty-two proprietors, including cotton gins, saloons, groceries, dance halls and opera houses, undertakers, doctors, and a candy store.

It was not until 1951 that the Felician Sisters of the Roman Catholic Church ran the newly constructed Yorktown Memorial Hospital. At the time, the closest hospital was about 75 miles north-west in San Antonio, Texas, and too far for most travelers. The funding to build the facility came from fundraising, donations, and grants from companies like the Ford Motor Company.

Stories report that over 500 patients died within six years and well over two thousand total deaths inside this one small hospital during its forty-year span. The building is around 30,000 sq. feet in size and holds a basement and two wings. The second floor had living quarters for employees.

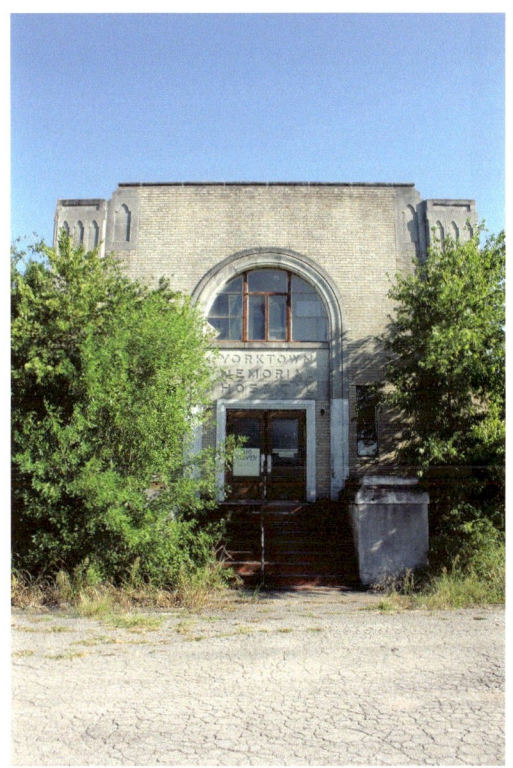

*Right:* Narrow corridors and bland, green walls give a haunted appearance to a rather plain building. (*Nicholas Henderson*)

*Below:* Over 2,000 deaths have occurred in the hospital. (*Nicholas Henderson*)

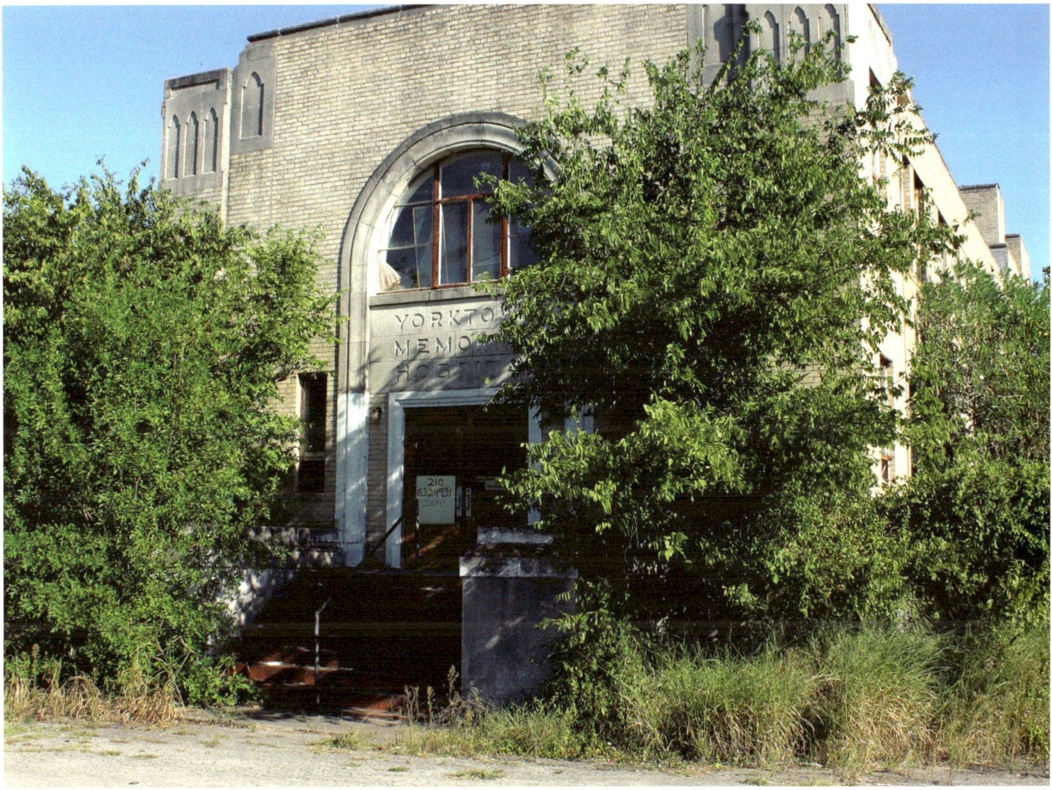

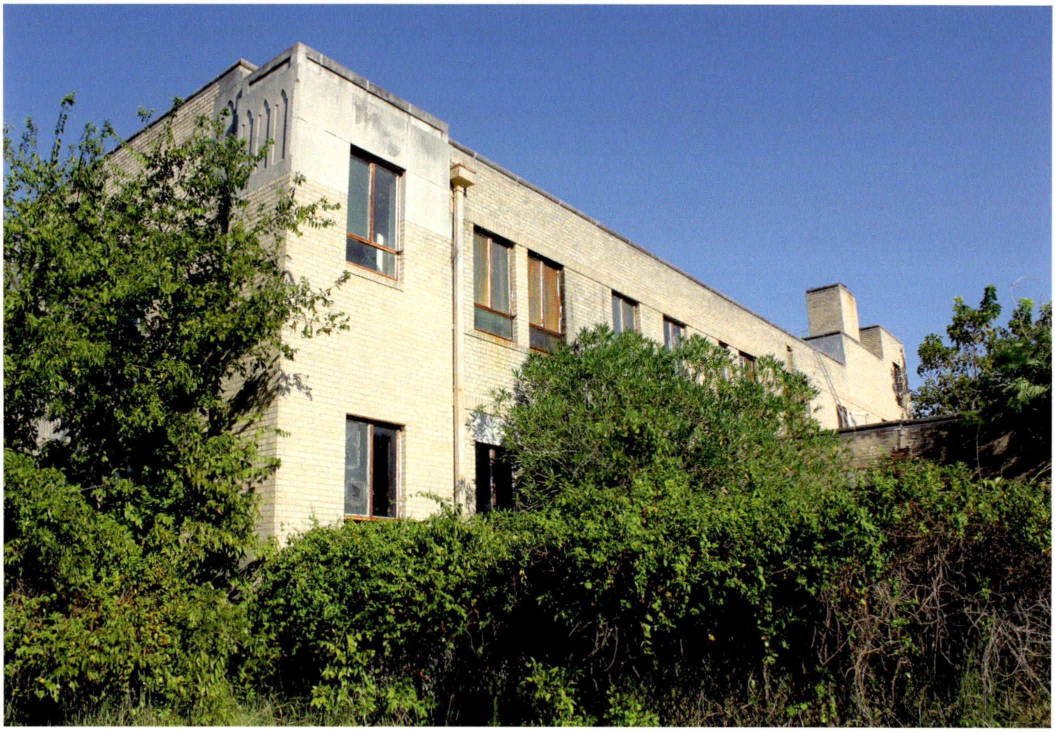

The building closed in 1992 and has sat vacant since that time. (*Nicholas Henderson*)

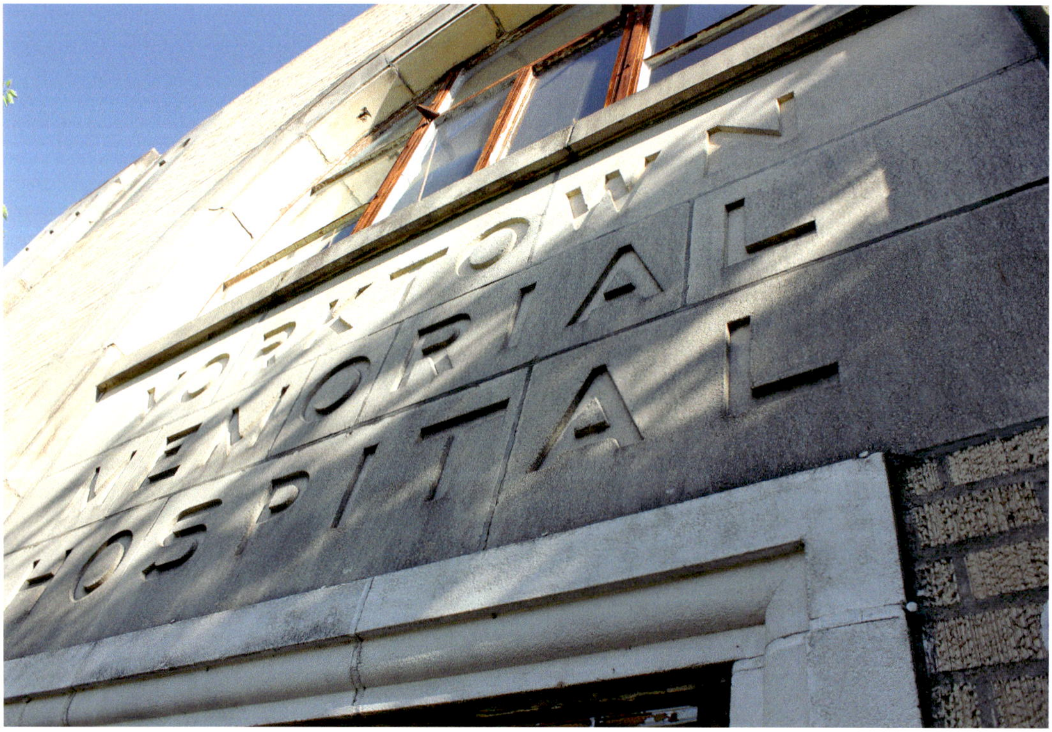

Yorktown Hospital was investigated by the Travel Channel's *Ghost Adventures*. (*Nicholas Henderson*)

The hospital closed in 1986 when a new, larger hospital opened in a neighboring town. The old building housed a drug rehabilitation center until 1992 and reached an officially decommissioned status.

Despite being a sizeable religious institute, the hospital had a bad reputation. Staff turnover resulted in a lack of continuity of care and poor standards. The low standards of care most likely led to exceedingly elevated death rates. Do the high death rates correlate with the copious ghost stories surrounding this abandoned building? Who are the reported ghosts? These questions sparked the interest of the *Ghost Adventures* crew and paranormal investigators from all over the state and country.

One medical provider who visitors state lingers behind to haunt Yorktown Memorial is Dr. Leon Nowierski, who worked at the hospital until after he turned ninety. Rumors report he was careless and possibly contributed to some of the deaths at Yorktown. By his retirement, he was the oldest working practitioner in Texas. However, there are no recorded cases of malpractice against Dr. Nowierski. Locals working on the oil rigs report frequent injuries, which can be severe. These large machines may contribute to the death toll. I am guessing Dr. Nowierski is still working at the hospital and caring for patients.

Visitors believe there is a young female spirit named Stacy. She is interactive and loves to be read to by visitors. A book, *The Poky Little Puppy*, is available and has a handwritten note from the person who provided Stacy with the book, Dr. Nowierski. She hangs out around one of the first-floor rooms but likes to explore the hallways

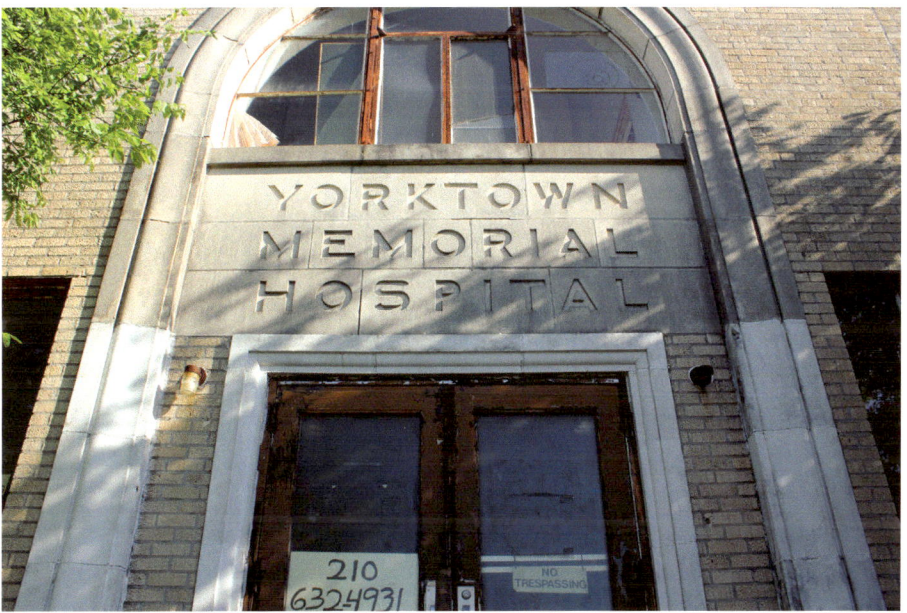

Little has been removed from the building, adding to the sealed-in-history feeling as visitors walk the halls. (*Nicholas Henderson*)

and basement. She is said to be friendly and enjoys rolling the ball back and forth if she is not listening to a story.

The nuns remain in the building. They were perhaps completing their duties as assigned by Dr. Nowierski. Some visitors claim that the nuns are violent and dislike tattoos. Blame for the sensation of being choked, scratched, or run over goes to the nuns. Photographers claim to have evidence of a nun wearing her habit.

Visitors named a male adult spirit Doug Richards. They feel Richards worked as a heavy equipment operator who perhaps worked on the oil rigs. He roams halls in blue jeans and a t-shirt. This description correlates with a man who died at the hospital in 1973.

When the hospital ran as a drug rehabilitation center, friends dropped off a young man overdosed on drugs. They rang the emergency bell and ran away, fearing they might be in trouble for using drugs. At least one nurse always stayed awake overnight, listening for the emergency bell. However, on that fateful night, everyone slept. The following morning staff found the young man's body. Visitors report a knocking noise around the back door and believe this could be the spirit of the young man or his friends attempting to get the staff's attention.

At least one homicide occurred in the hospital's basement when it operated as a drug rehabilitation center. The stories vary, but it always comes back to two men and one female. It may have been two nurses, one patient, or two nurses. Both accounts detail a woman caught in the broiler room. She and one of the men were in a compromising position. The second man stabbed the woman repeatedly until she died. The first man wrestled the knife away from the attacker and stabbed him to death. Blood splatter remains on the walls today. The caregiver of the building reports that the marks on the wall were forensically tested and positive for human blood.

Instead, it is the known spirits, a scream from the obstetric department, moaning from the emergency area, or shadows roaming the halls that form the paranormal evidence presenting itself to visitors. Even *Ghost Adventures* investigated the hospital and obtained evidence. They found audio evidence, including rattles, bangs, and voices, felt cold spots, and Zak Bagans agitated the nuns with his tattoos. The electronic voice phenomenon *Ghost Adventures* collected includes:

"You wanna play?"
"It must be told, and I'll tell them."
"It's sick."
"Don't go in the bathroom."
"Okay."
"Get in there."
"The killer is coming. Get in the hallway."

## Old Yoakum Community Hospital

Construction began in 1887 when the San Antonio and Aransas Pass Railway vice president laid out the new roundhouse and maintenance shop structure. The action brought business to the town and employed hundreds of workers.

The first community hospital arrived in 1922 thanks to the donation of land and money from the late John Huth. Huth Community Hospital served the town of Yoakum and the surrounding area. The city of Yoakum owned and operated the hospital until 1933. The depression and decline of the economy forced the city to sell to the Sisters of the Incarnate Word and Blessed Sacrament of Victoria. The area thrived for many years, and the population increased. The small hospital was abandoned in 1997 when a larger, more modern facility replaced the original hospital.

The paranormal group, Old Yoakum Community Hospital Group, manages the building and conducts investigations in the vacated building. They also lease the building to other paranormal investigation teams to keep the documentation of events.

On the night of March 6, 1990, Gregory Hights stormed into Yoakum Community Hospital, angered by the belief that his wife, Laura, was cheating. Laura worked as a nurse and greeted him in the waiting room. She had no idea of the tragic events that would leave a mark on history. A fight ensued. Gregory shot Laura in the head at point-blank range. Laura's co-workers raced to her aid, but she died in the intensive care unit where she once worked. Gregory took his own life in jail just five months following his arrest.

Investigators believe Laura reaches out to them via spikes on their EMP detectors. At least once, a full apparition of a woman has appeared.

Another possible spirit is Father Charles Kram, who served as a hospital chaplain for over twenty-five years. At the age of twenty-three, Kram contracted paralytic polio and became paralyzed from the neck down. He spent several months in an iron lung. After months of rehabilitation, Kram learned to use devices to feed himself and write. He kept control of his wheelchair with a ball-covered stem that rested just under his chin. Kram's presence at the hospital blessed and touched many visitors. Father Kram passed away in 2000, but many believe he still faithfully moves through the hospital, blessing everyone.

Father Kram's original wheelchair remains in the chapel, and investigators believe they have encountered his presence in the chapel and office.

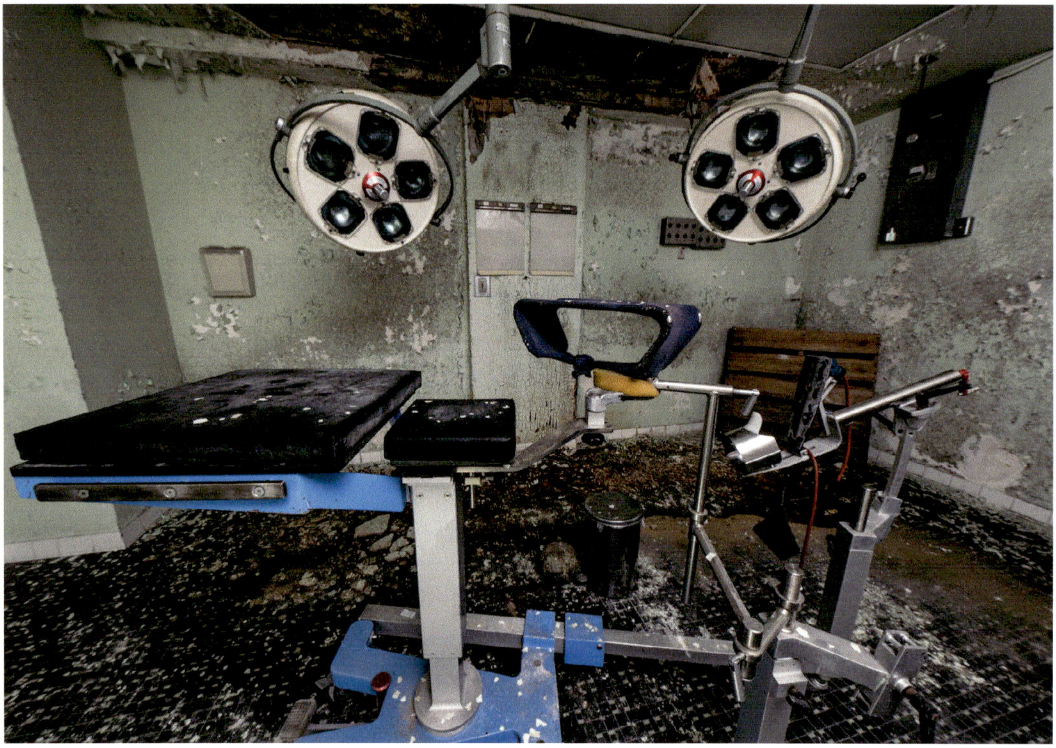

The Huth Community Hospital was opened in 1922. (*Kevin Lynch*)

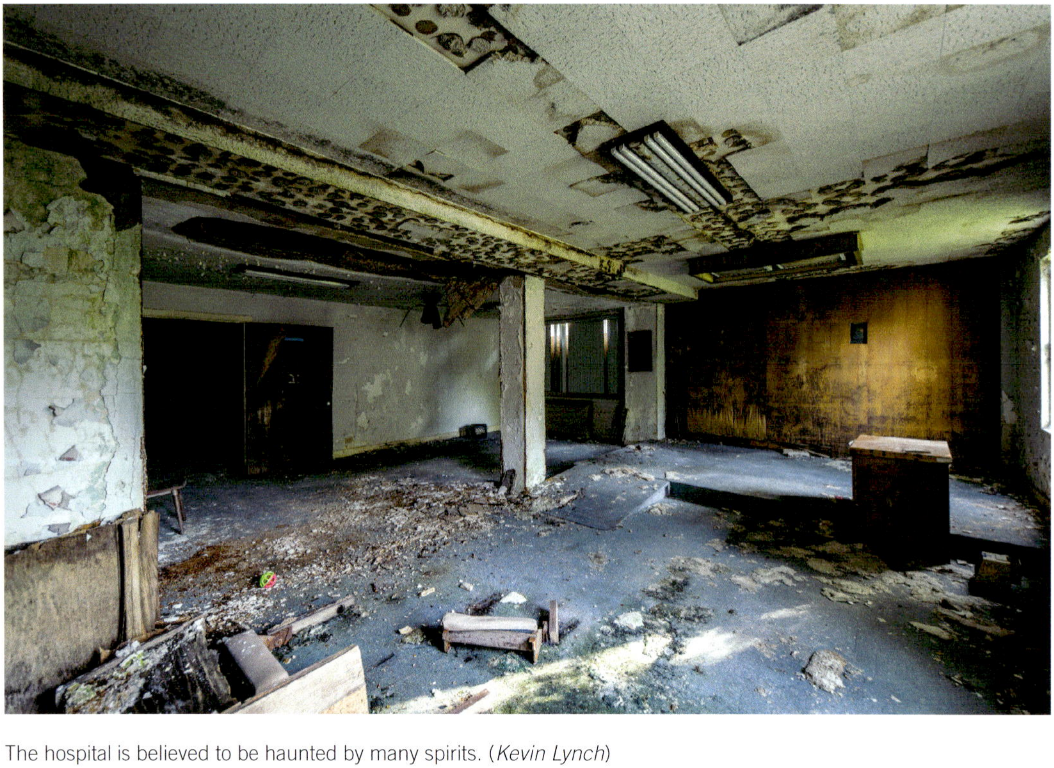

The hospital is believed to be haunted by many spirits. (*Kevin Lynch*)

## Maxdale Bridge and Cemetery

In July 1913, the Bell County Commissioner's Court approved the construction of the Maxdale bridge. The area floods, which blocked access for travelers. During construction, a flood occurred and destroyed the first attempt at building a bridge over the waterway of the Lampasas River. Engineers went back to work and completed the steel truss construction in 1914.

Not too far from the bridge is the Maxdale Cemetery, established in 1863. The cemetery is one of the oldest in Bell County, with nearly 400 graves. Frank McBryde, Sr., donated the land. His 1883 application for a post office for the community resulted in the name changing to Maxdale. The earliest documented grave belonged to Lousia Marlar in 1868.

While it was challenging to locate the exact date that the bridge closed to motorized traffic, it appears to be around the same time it became a historical landmark in 1990. It is not challenging to locate ghost stories surrounding the bridge and cemetery.

One story states that a man attempted to save his girlfriend from drowning in the water. He tied a noose and hung himself from the Maxdale Bridge when he failed. Legend states that visitors who park, facing the bridge, turn off their headlights, count to ten, and then turn the light back on will see a ghostly figure having from a noose. Another possible spirit is a young woman holding flowers and wearing a long, white dress as she floats down the river. The story matches the original tale of a young woman who died in the river.

Another story reports that a bus filled with children had a fatal accident and crashed into the river below. Those who park their cars near the bridge find tiny handprints in the dust.

The former caretaker walks with a definitive limp and roams the cemetery at night.

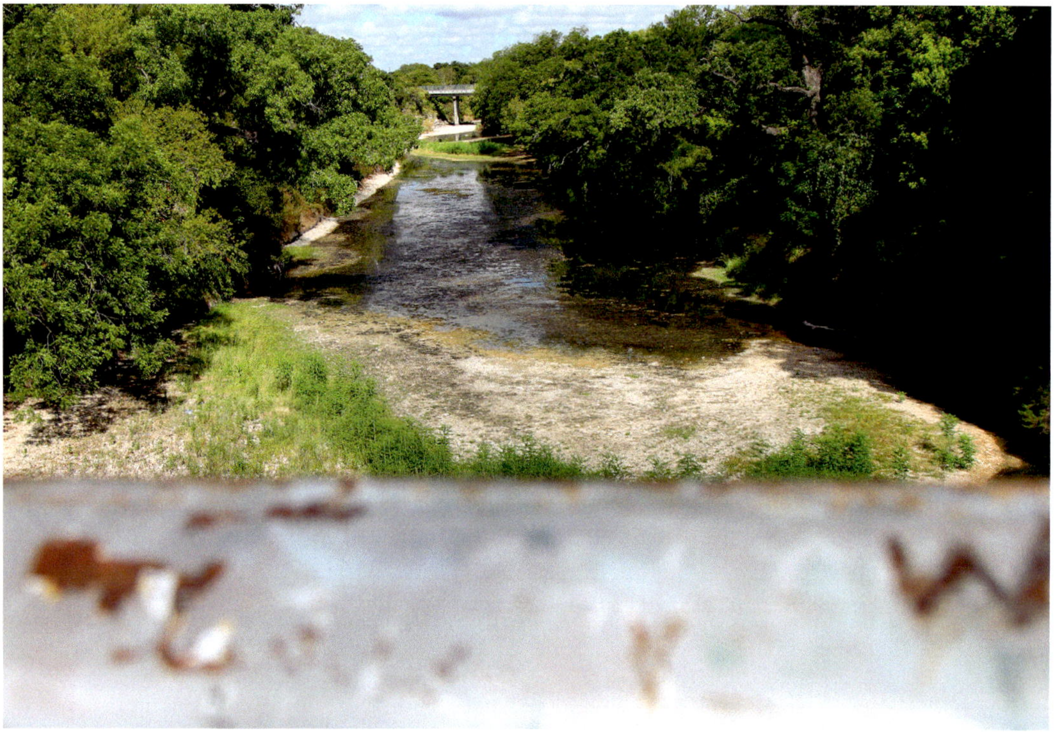

The Maxdale Bridge spans over murky, muddy waters. (*Larry Moore*)

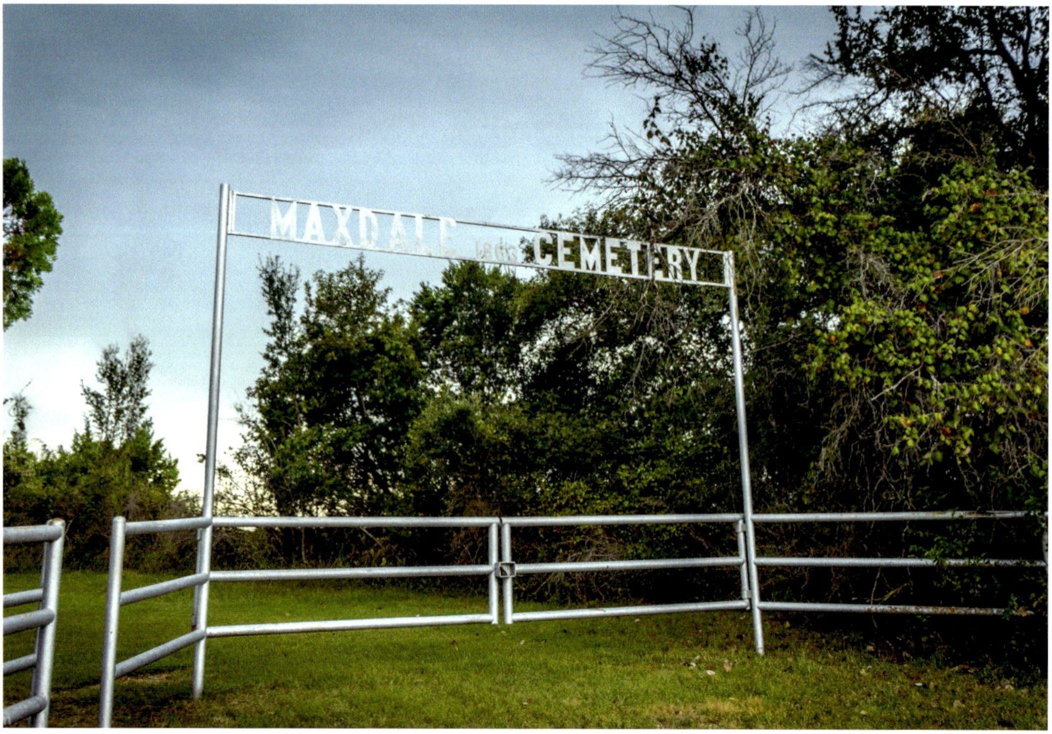

The Maxdale Cemetery is just down the road from the bridge. (*Kevin Lynch*)

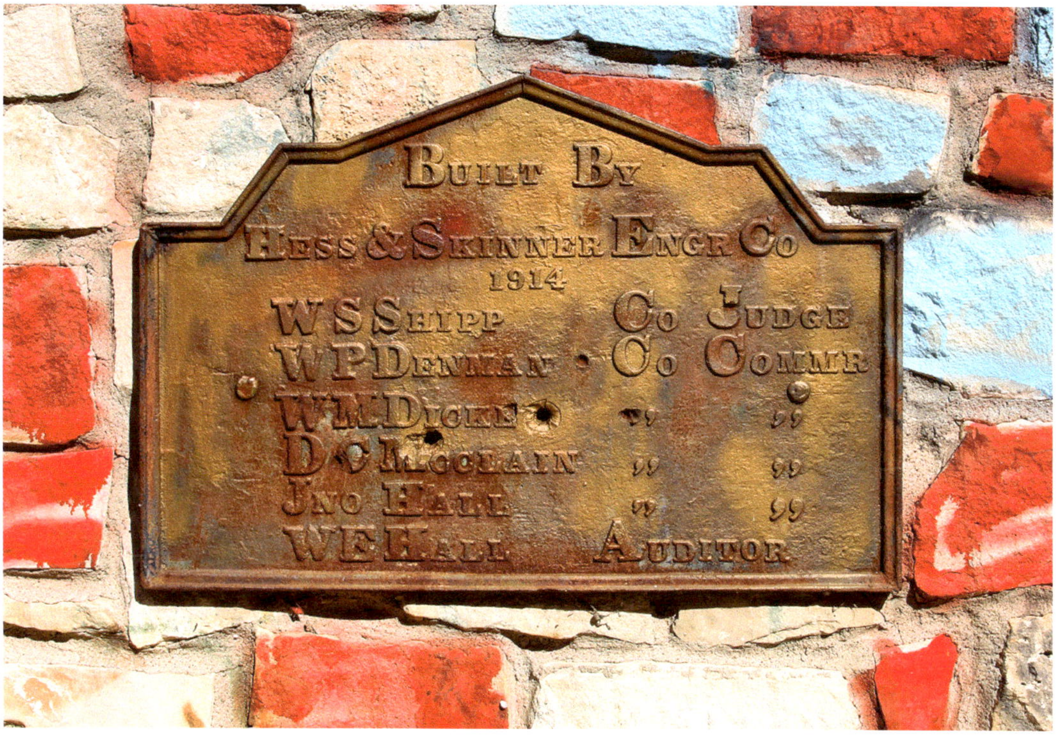

An old, rusty sign makes the historical bridge. (*Larry Moore*)

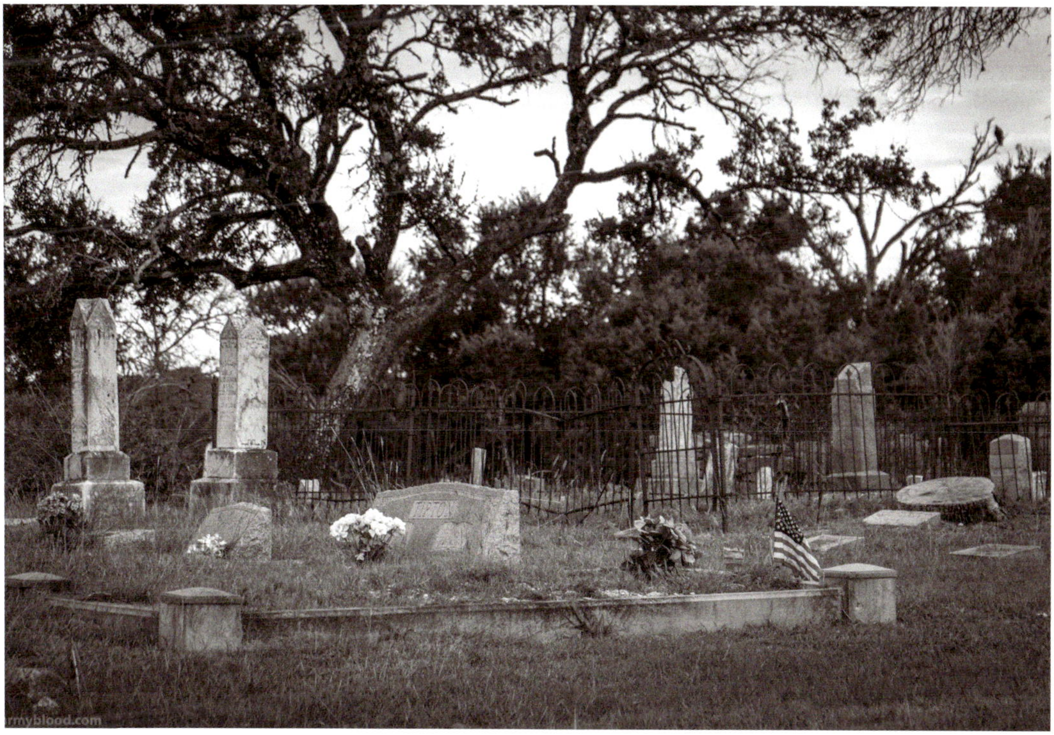

Rust begins to eat away at the metal trusses of the bridge. (*Kevin Lynch*)

# 4

# DESERTED DESTINATIONS

A ghost town is an abandoned town, city, or village usually containing several remnants of structures. They derive when economic activity has failed and natural or human-caused disasters.

## Terlingua, Texas

Terlingua, Texas, along the Rio Grande River, began as a mining town in the state's southern region. Around the mid-1880s, settlers discovered a cinnamon-red stone known as cinnabar. The brilliant, scarlet red stone is adorned for use in pottery and is the most common source of ore for mercury.

Jack Dawson produced the first mercury from Terlingua in 1888. However, it was not publicized and formally mined until around 1900. Howard Perry, a Cleveland and Chicago businessman, acquired four sections of land in Texas as payment for an unpaid debt, winnings from a poker game. To Perry, this land was a desert wasteland until he began receiving offers to purchase the land at a significant increase. Perry discovered the valuable mineral held a hefty price tag, and being an astute businessman, he staked claim to his land and the cinnabar. He traveled to Almaden, Spain, to study the world's most successful mercury mine. In 1903, he returned to the United States, created the Chisos Mining Company in the area, and began harvesting cinnabar for mercury production.

Historians report Perry had the ethics of a pirate and did not bat an eye when he smuggled in Mexican workers to provide cheap labor for his mines which contained some of the richest deposits in the area. These workers experienced dangerous

# TERLINGUA, TEXAS

TERLINGUA, TEXAS (ALTITUDE 3000') IS LOCATED MORE THAN 10 MILES NORTH OF THE RIO GRANDE IN THE BIG BEND REGION. THE TOWN IS NAMED FOR NEARBY TERLINGUA CREEK, WHICH FLOWS FROM THE HIGHLANDS SOUTH INTO THE RIO GRANDE JUST BELOW THE POINT WHERE THE RIVER WIDENS AND SLOWS BEYOND THE FURIOUS WHITEWATER OF THE SANTA ELENA CANYON. TERLINGUA OWES ITS EXISTENCE TO THE DISCOVERY THERE OF LARGE QUICKSILVER (OR MERCURY) DEPOSITS, THE BI-PRODUCT OF ANCIENT VOLCANIC ACTION.

ALTHOUGH IT HAD LONG BEEN RUMORED THAT THERE WAS QUICKSILVER IN THE HILLS, AND IT WAS COMMON KNOWLEDGE THAT THE INDIANS OF THE AREA USED CINNEBAR, OR QUICKSILVER ORE, AS PAINT FOR WAR AND THE PEACEFUL ARTS, IT WAS NOT UNTIL JUST BEFORE THE TURN OF THE CENTURY THAT AMERICANS AND MEXICANS BEGAN MOVING INTO THE AREA IN SERIOUS QUEST FOR MINING OPPORTUNITIES. HOWARD E. PERRY, A BUSINESSMAN WITH INTERESTS FROM MAINE TO TEXAS WAS ONE OF THE FIRST. EARLY ON THE QUICKSILVER INDUSTRY BENEFITED WHEN TERLINGUA ORE WAS PRESENTED AT THE ST. LOUIS WORLD'S FAIR IN 1910. ALTHOUGH FOURTEEN OTHER MINES WERE ESTABLISHED IN THE AREA BEFORE AND AFTER THE CHISOS MINE, IT WAS THE MOST SUCCESSFUL AND REMAINED IN OPERATION UNTIL 1946.

TODAY TERLINGUA STANDS AS A GHOST TOWN. DESIGNATED AS AN HISTORIC SITE BY THE STATE, IT WELCOMES TOURISTS TODAY. RONNIE C. TYLER, CURATOR OF HISTORY AT THE AMON CARTER MUSEUM OF WESTERN ART IN FORT WORTH, DESCRIBES THE HOWARD E. PERRY HOUSE TODAY: "LOCATED ON A HILL OVER LOOKING THE VILLAGE, THIS STURDY, TWO-STORY BUILDING IS SYMBOLIC OF WHAT HAS HAPPENED IN TERLINGUA. FROM THE FRONT PORCH ONE CAN SEE THE DESERTED MINE SHAFTS THAT BROUGHT HUNDREDS OF WORKERS TO THE BIG BEND AREA EARLY IN THE CENTURY, AND IN THE DISTANCE, SANTA ELENA CANYON AND THE CHISOS MOUNTAINS, THE IMPRESSIVE LANDSCAPE WHICH ATTRACTS VISITORS TODAY."

THE DOCUMENTATION OF TERLINGUA, TEXAS WAS UNDERTAKEN BY THE WASHINGTON, D.C. OFFICE OF THE HISTORIC AMERICAN BUILDINGS SURVEY (HABS) AND WAS SPONSORED BY THE TEXAS HISTORICAL COMMISSION, AND BIG BEND NATIONAL PARK.

THE 1985 SUMMER DOCUMENTATION PROJECT WAS CONDUCTED BY THE HABS/HAER DIVISION, AND WAS ORGANIZED AND DIRECTED BY KENNETH L. ANDERSON, PRINCIPAL ARCHITECT OF HABS IN CONJUNCTION WITH JOE OPPERMAN, DEPUTY STATE HISTORIC PRESERVATION OFFICER, TEXAS HISTORICAL COMMISSION AND GILBERT LUSK, SUPERINTENDENT, BIG BEND NATIONAL PARK.

THE 1985 ARCHITECTURAL DOCUMENTATION OF TERLINGUA WAS PRODUCED BY PROJECT SUPERVISOR DANIEL WININSKY (PENNSYLVANIA STATE UNIVERSITY) AND ARCHITECTURE TECHNICIANS JOSEPH BALACHOWSKI (CALIFORNIA POLYTECHNICAL UNIVERSITY), PAMELA MATHIS (TULANE UNIVERSITY), AND DOUGLAS LISTER (TULANE UNIVERSITY).

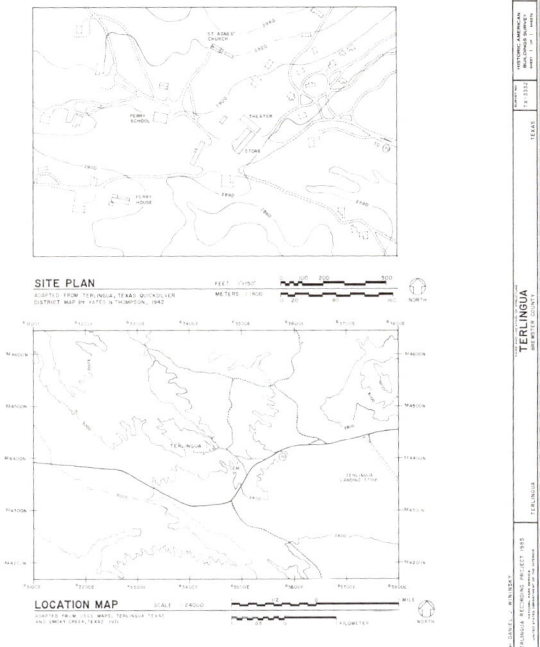

*Above:* Chisos Mining Company filed for bankruptcy in 1942, causing the mine to close and the town to die. (*Library of Congress*)

*Right:* Terlingua was established in 1899. (*Carol Highsmith*)

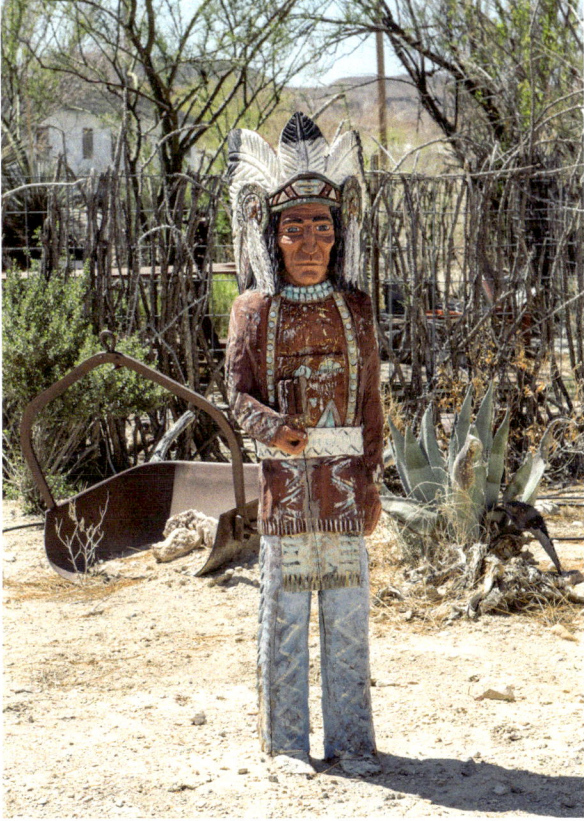

conditions in the mines and worked long hours, sometimes seven days a week, for little pay. The only employee benefit was free housing in meager accommodations made from stone.

Perry's business flourished three years later, and he set plans to construct a mansion for himself and his bride. The estate took form on a hill, high above the mining caves. The majestic home featured nine bedrooms, a wine cellar, and a 90-foot front porch adorned with elegant arches. With the mansion complete, Perry called for his wife. The Chicago native traveled for days to reach the Texas desert, but after just one day, she demanded to leave. Perry could also return to Chicago and run his mining operation remotely. He occasionally visited the mansion and kept an eye on his crew.

As the mine prospered, Perry added to the town of Terlingua. The first addition was a company store where the miners received their paychecks and supplies. Over time, he said, an ice-making plant, a cantina, a hotel, schools, an ice-cream shop, a church, a theater, a post office, and a jail. The cemetery in Terlingua built itself. The town grew to around 2,000 in the population at its highest.

All good things must come to an end. By 1943, the world's mercury supply was abundant, and the value decreased. The Chisos Mining Company ended in bankruptcy. Howard Perry died the following year.

Today restoration efforts have focused on the Perry mansion and preserving this small piece of Texas history. Most of the mining company's buildings are in ruins. The general store is still operational for tourists. The cemetery photographs so well that it is one of the most photographed in the state. The current population is around fifty-eight, but visitors feel many of the miners have never left and still float through the ghost town.

Visitors to Terlingua often report blackouts, blurred vision, and even hallucinations. Could this be the spirits of miners reaching out to the living and expressing the sensations that they experienced in the dark mines? One researcher stated that the area puts out low-frequency sound waves, which could create these anomalies and deteriorate the mental health of those who remain in Terlingua.

## Barstow, Texas

George Barstow developed land in Texas and is known as a pioneer in irrigation. In 1891, he gathered with other land developers to promote a town on the Texas Pacific Railway. The Texas Pacific Railway Company arrived via a federal chapter in 1871 to build a railroad connecting Marshall, Texas, to San Diego, California. By

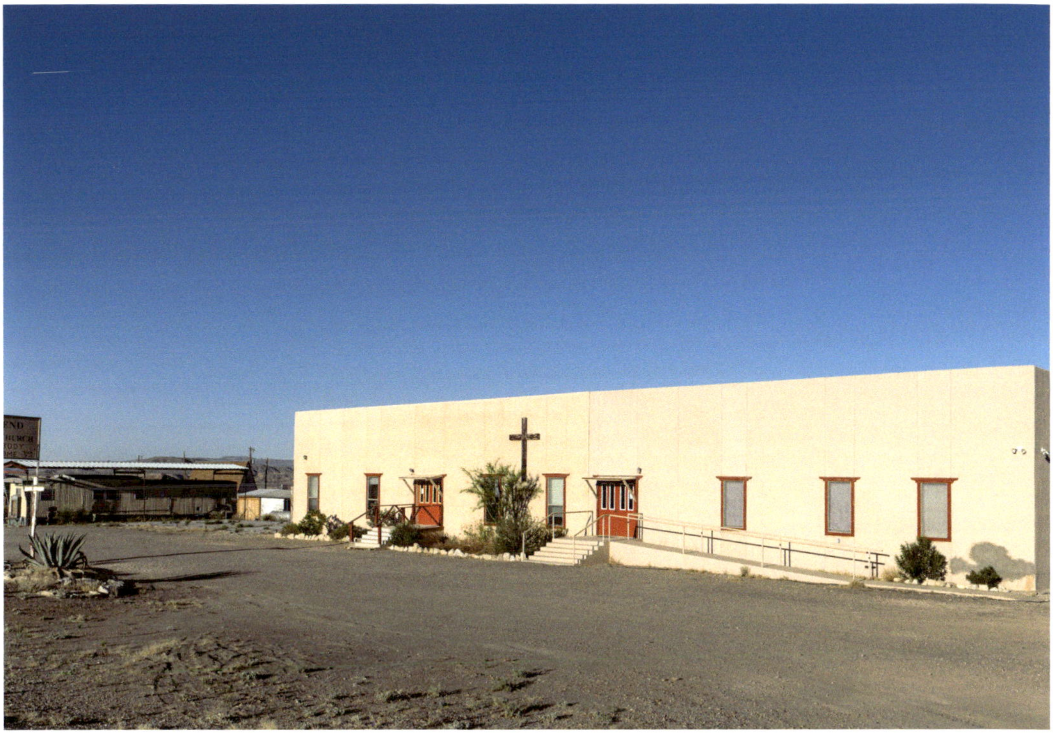

Cinnabar, a rich-mercury sulfide, was discovered. (*Carol Highsmith*)

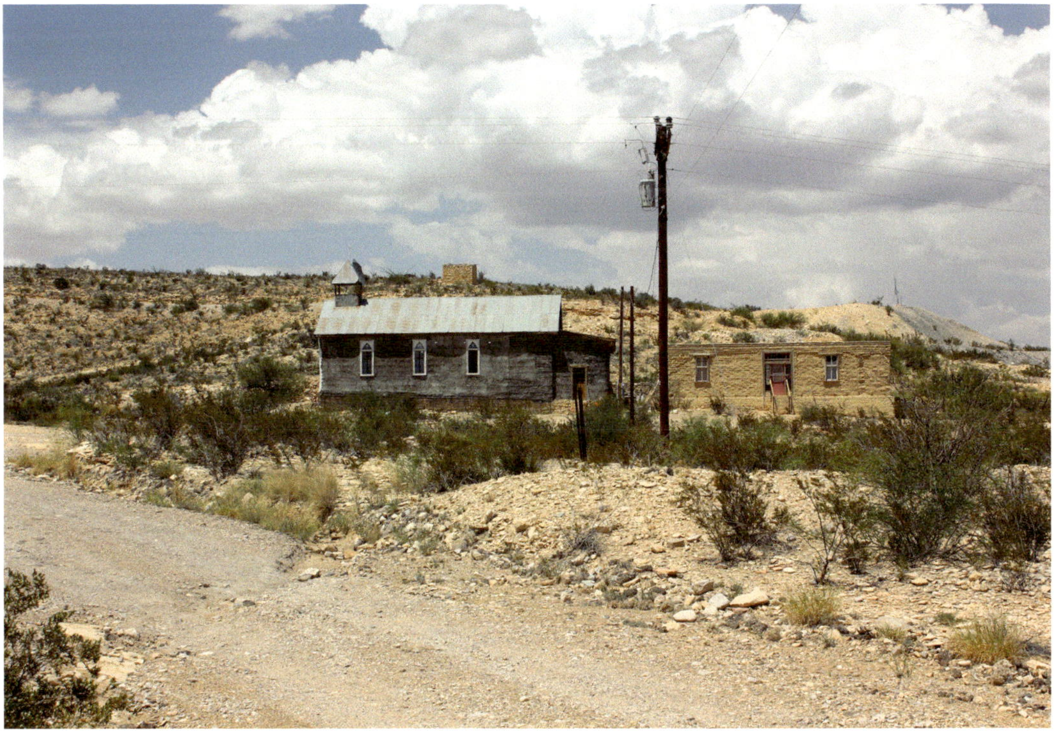

The town grew to over 2,000 citizens as the mining industry did well. (*Carol Highsmith*)

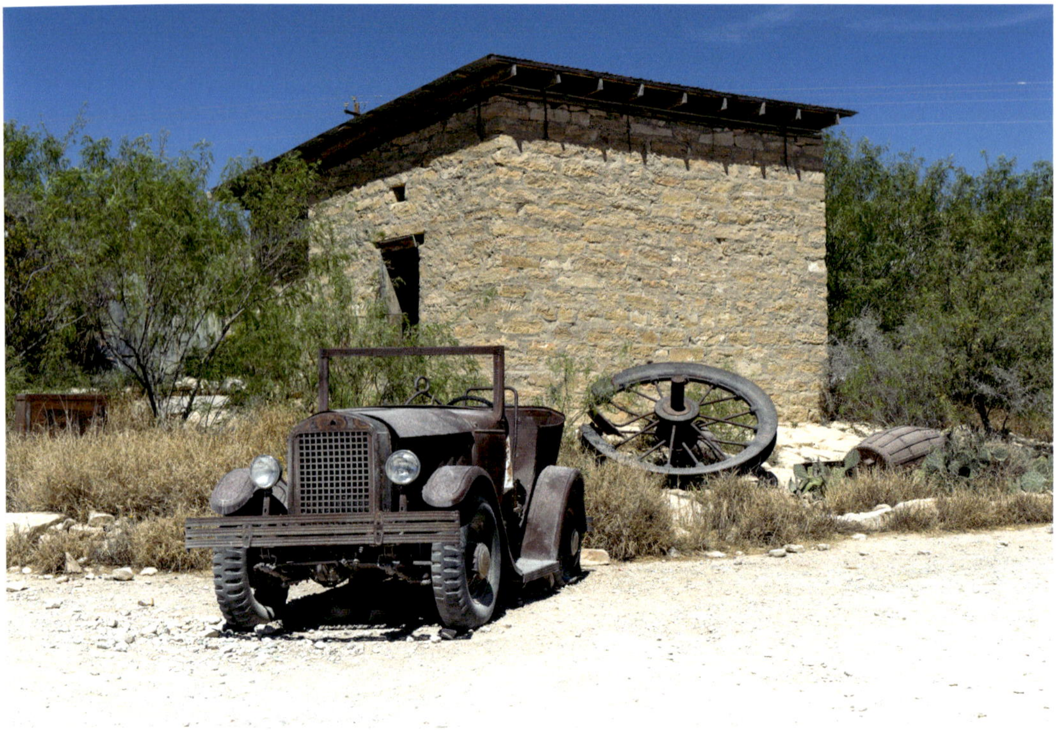

By 1926, 40 percent of the cinnabar was mined. (*Carol Highsmith*)

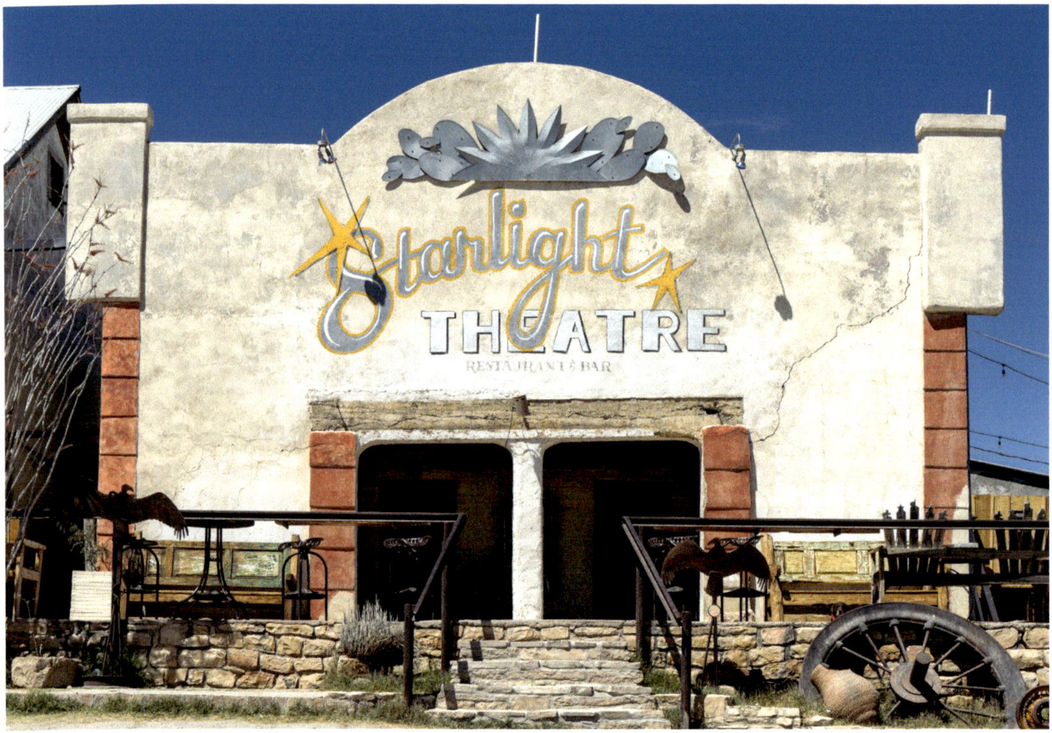

In addition to the mine, the town had temporary housing for about 200 to 300 workers. (*Carol Highsmith*)

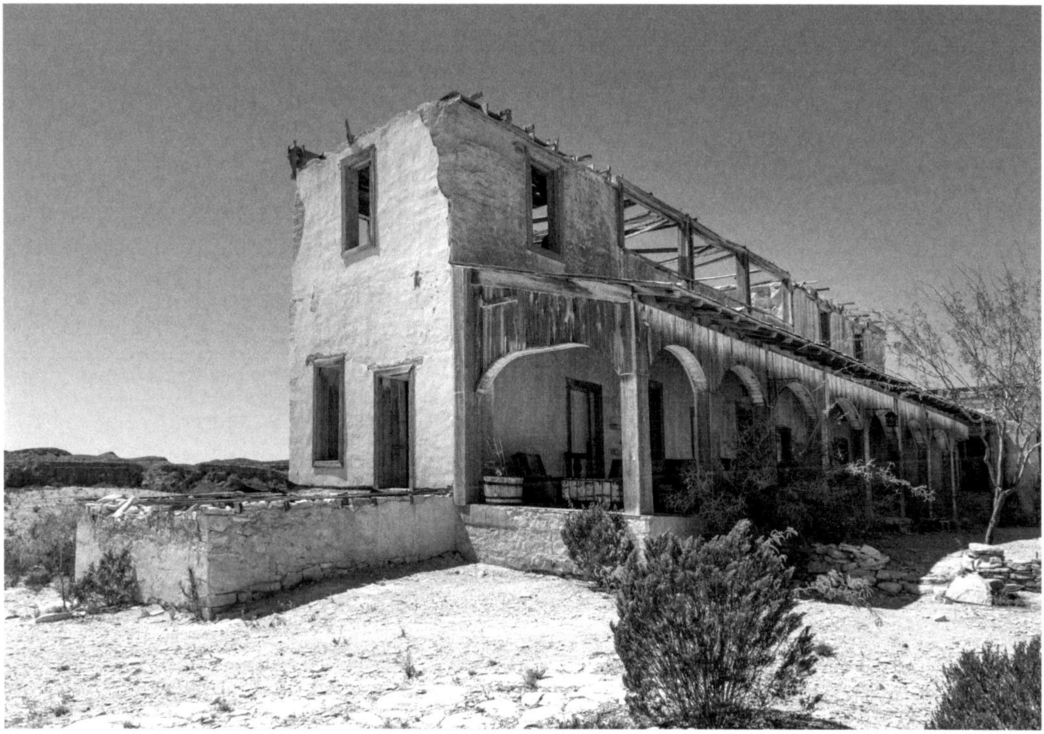

Terlingua was a segregated town with Mexican families in one area. (*Carol Highsmith*)

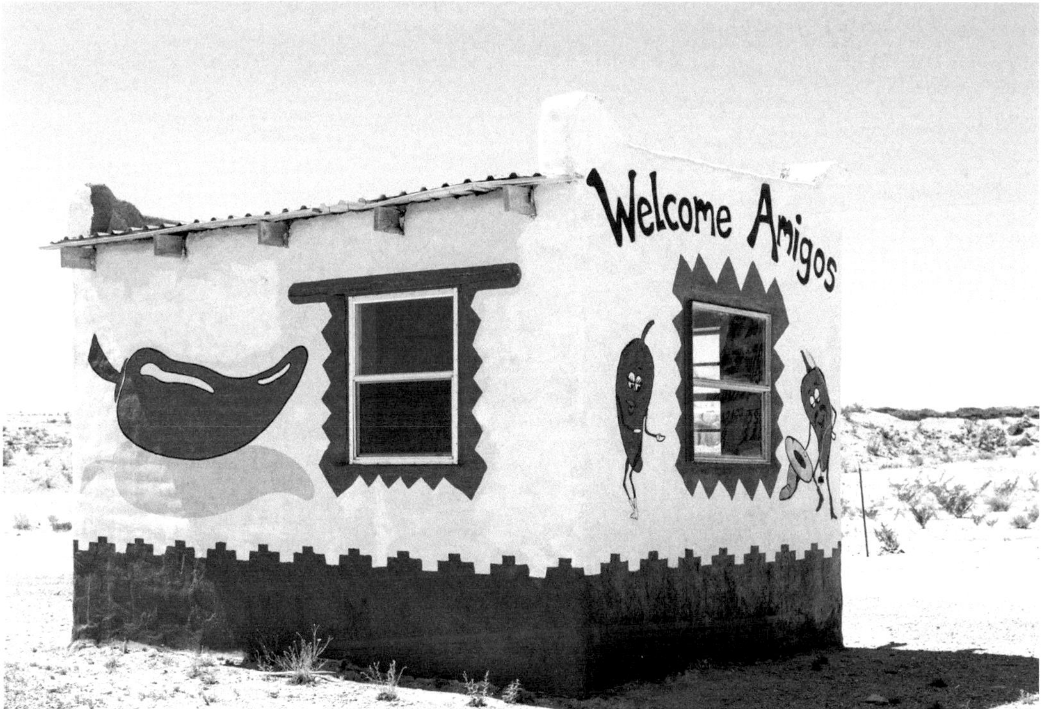

Howard Perry, the owner of the mine, built a mansion on the property in around 1910. (*Carol Highsmith*)

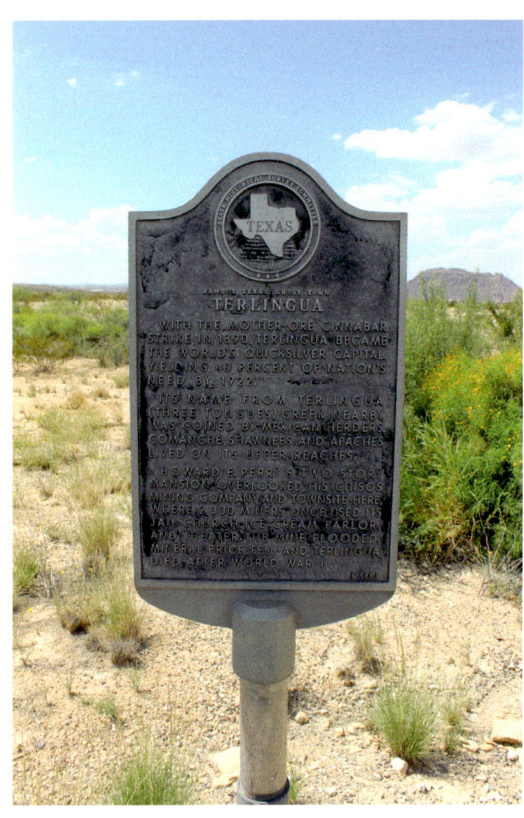

*Left:* Many deaths occurred due to mercury poisoning. (*Carol Highsmith*)

*Below:* There is a graveyard without 400 souls. (*Carol Highsmith*)

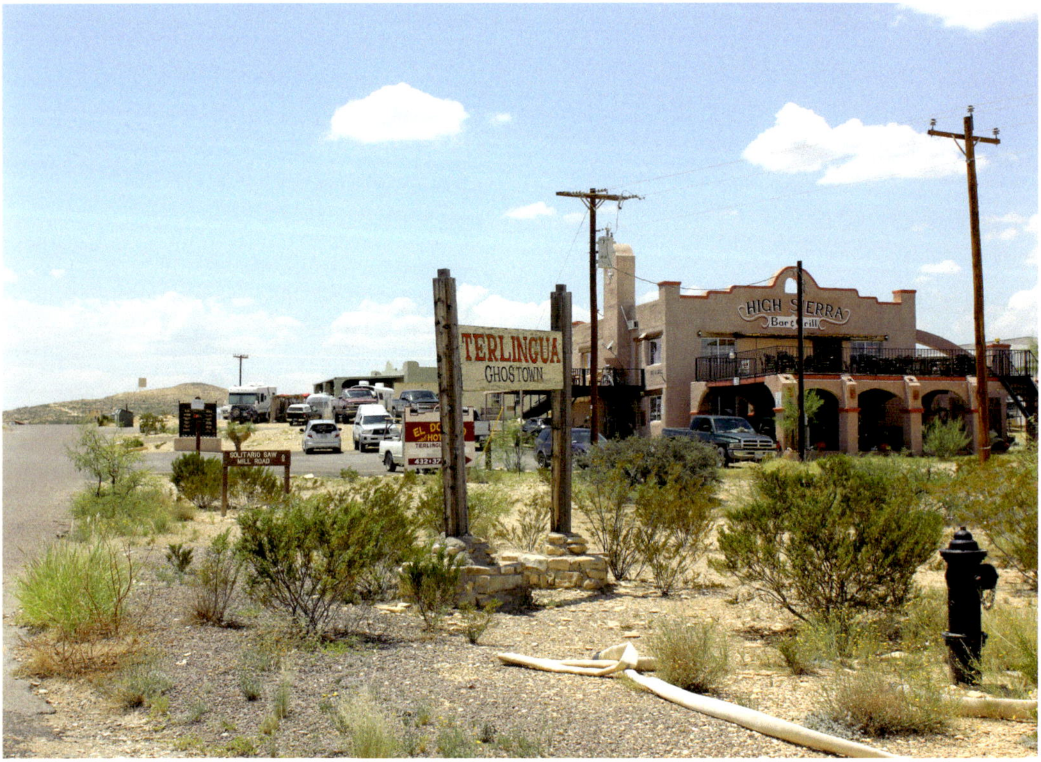

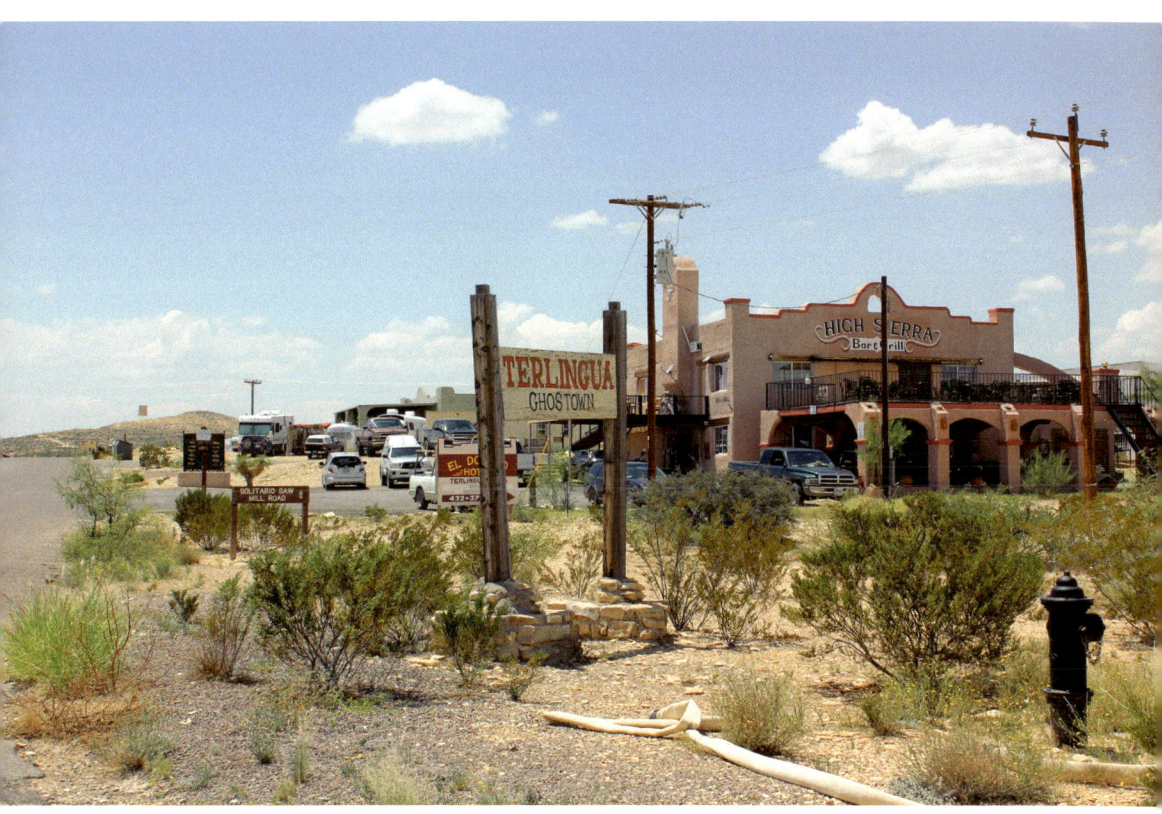

Terlingua was officially abandoned in the 1940s. (*Nicholas Henderson*)

1891, the town took the name Barstow. This plot of land was just 5 miles from the Pecos River, which would supply the city's irrigation.

Barstow grew with farming and agriculture thanks to the irrigation systems placed by Barstow. The farms in the area flourished with grapes, peaches, pears, and melons. However, in 1904, the Pecos River Dam broke, and drought came year after year. By 1918, farming was impossible, and the population of Barstow reached a dry spell.

## Independence, Texas

Founded in 1835, Independence, Texas, became the Republic of Texas's religious and educational center. That same year, Frances Trask started a boarding school for girls; by 1839, the Independence Baptist Church. In 1845, the delegates of the Union Baptist Association voted to adopt Reverend William Tryon and Robert Baylor's idea of establishing a Baptist university in Texas. At the time, Baylor was a district judge, former Congressman, and soldier. Three years later, the first site

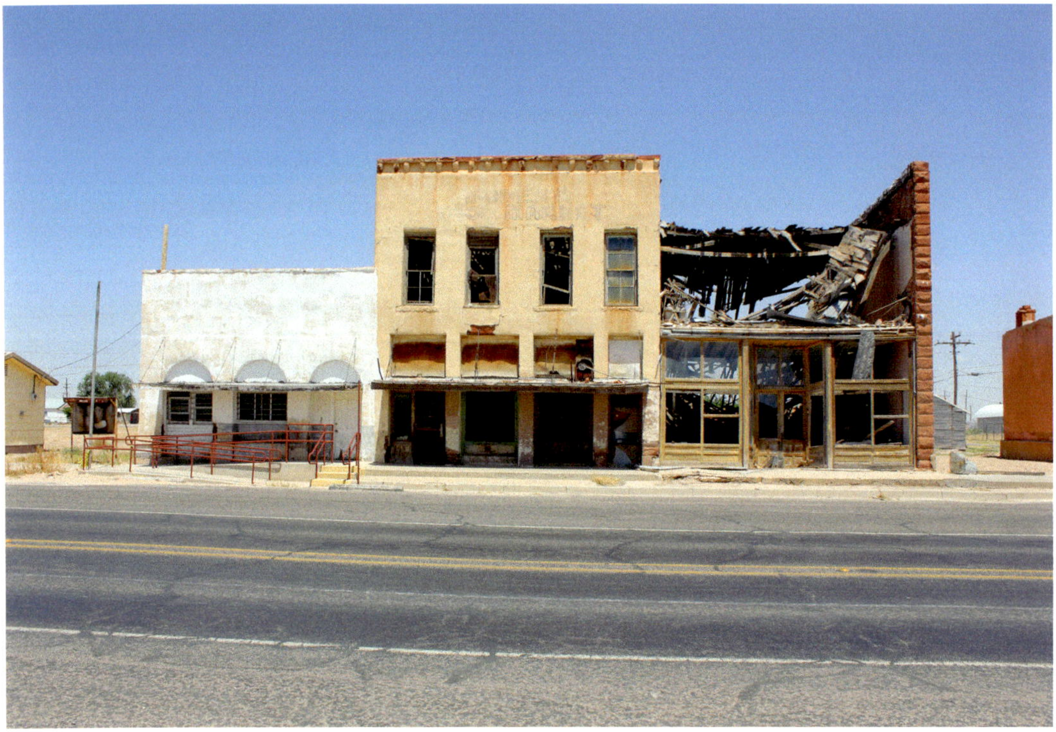

Barstow was established in 1892 and, by 2010, had only 310 remaining residents. (*Nicholas Henderson*)

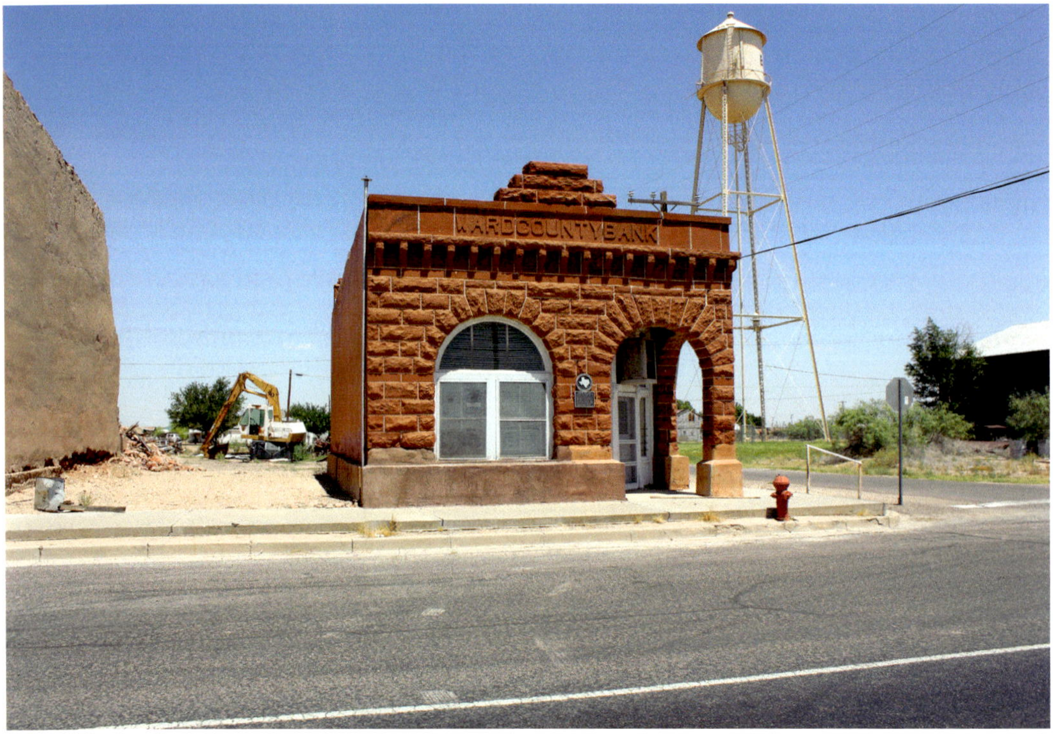

George Barstow was the world's leading person to work on irrigations system. (*Nicholas Henderson*)

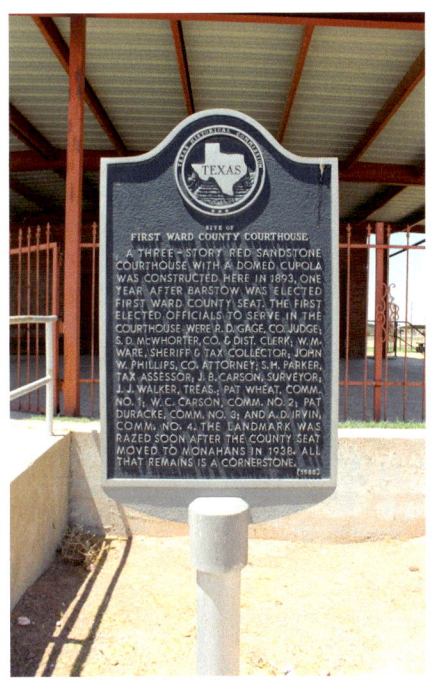
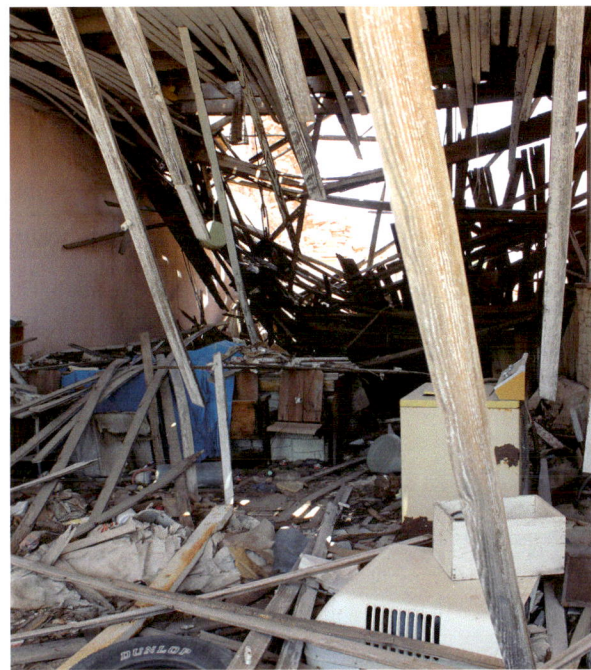

*Above left:* In 1918, farming was next to impossible due to the lack of water. (*Nicholas Henderson*)

*Above right:* The building in Barstow remains despite extensive damages. (*Nicholas Henderson*)

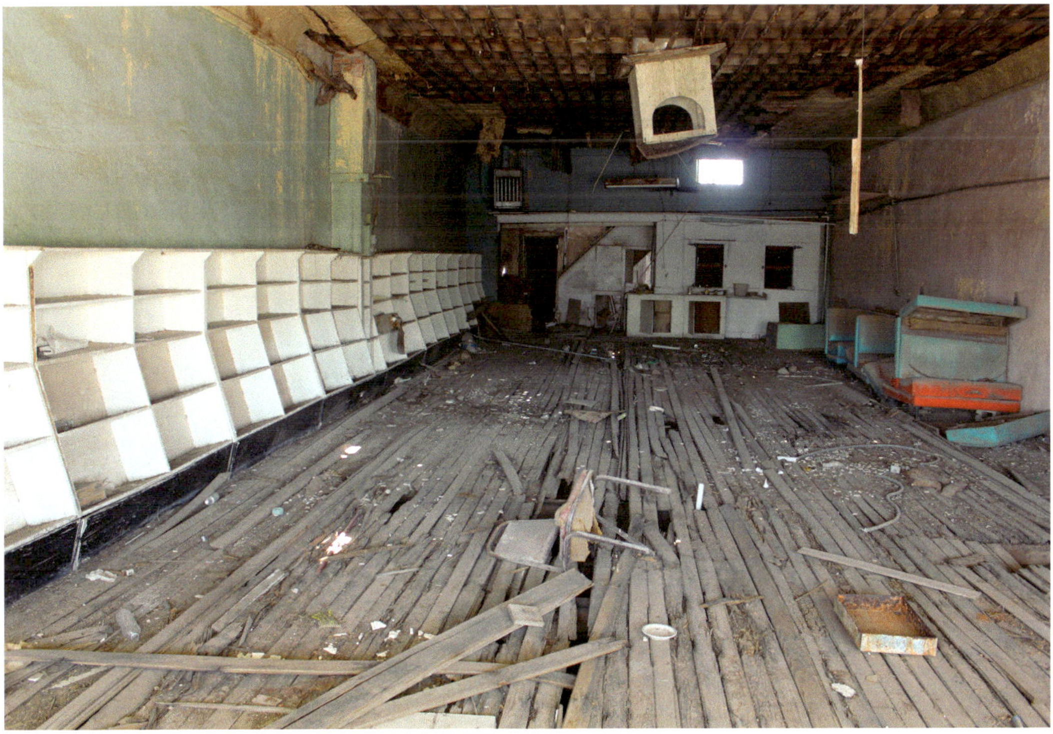

The interior of this building is no longer safe for people to investigate. (*Nicholas Henderson*)

of Baylor University and the University of Mary Hardin-Baylor came to life, making Independence the wealthiest town in Texas.

It did not take long for new citizens to flock to Independence. The town was incorporated in 1852 and established its first mayor. Soon after, settlers constructed a hotel, Masonic Lodge, a stagecoach depot, and a small commercial center. With such a strong foundation, this town drew prominent citizens like Sam Houston and William Bizzell.

The Santa Fe Railroad petitioned for the right-of-way to establish a line through town, but city officials refused. By the 1880s, this created a problem for trade and transportation. Historians blame the fall of Independence on the lack of a railroad. The lack of a railroad led to the loss of the universities. Baylor University officials decided to move both campuses away from Independence. With such a significant loss, the town suffered; by 1966, it held only around 200 residents.

Today, four pillars from the women's college, University of Mary Hardin-Baylor, remain among the ruins. A local legend states that a woman who lived in Independence belonged to a Satanic cult and decided to sacrifice her life for Satan. They believe she completed this task by climbing the old pillars of the university and hanging herself. Thus, placing a curse on the town and frequent reports of a woman dressed in a long black dress and veil floating around the pillars at night.

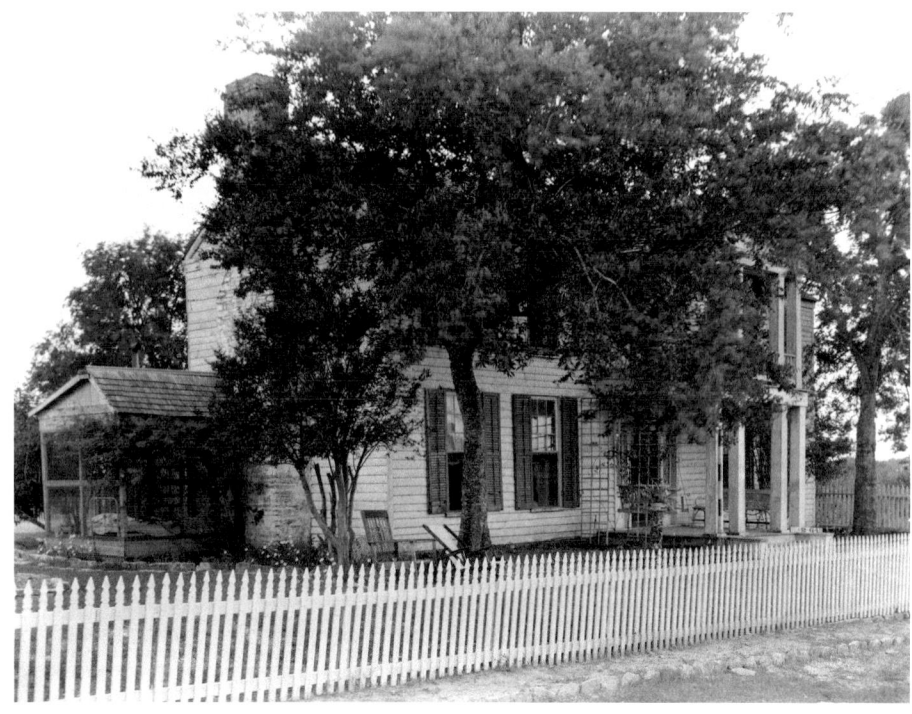

Independence was the location of the original campus of Baylor University. (*Library of Congress*)

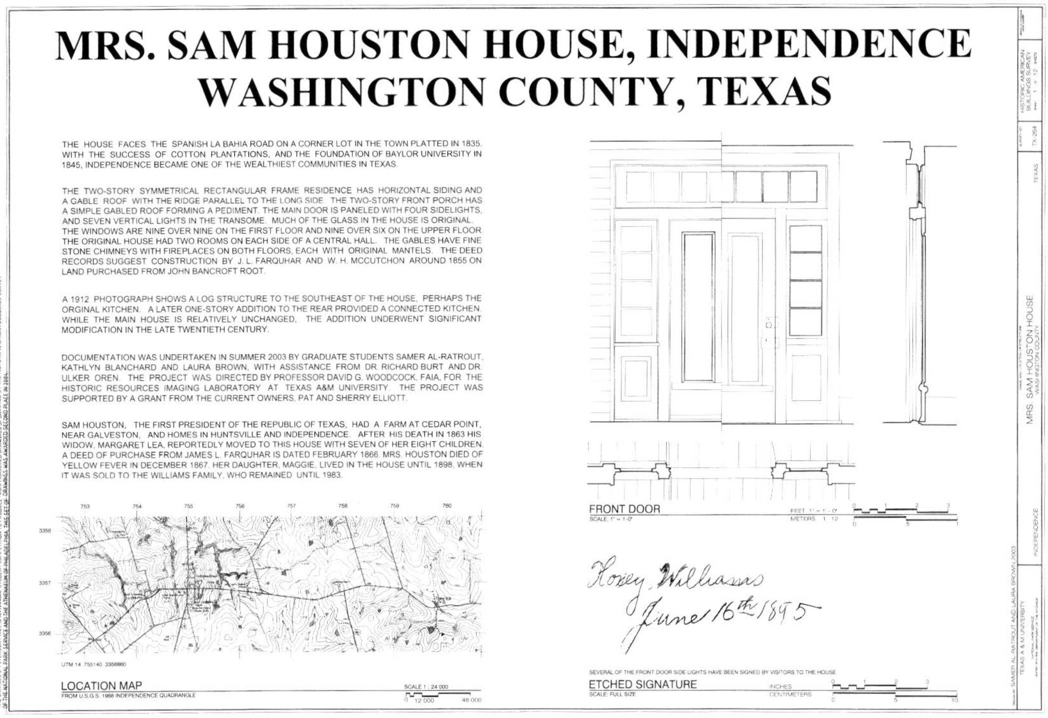

# MRS. SAM HOUSTON HOUSE, INDEPENDENCE WASHINGTON COUNTY, TEXAS

THE HOUSE FACES THE SPANISH LA BAHIA ROAD ON A CORNER LOT IN THE TOWN PLATTED IN 1835. WITH THE SUCCESS OF COTTON PLANTATIONS, AND THE FOUNDATION OF BAYLOR UNIVERSITY IN 1845, INDEPENDENCE BECAME ONE OF THE WEALTHIEST COMMUNITIES IN TEXAS.

THE TWO-STORY SYMMETRICAL RECTANGULAR FRAME RESIDENCE HAS HORIZONTAL SIDING AND A GABLE ROOF WITH THE RIDGE PARALLEL TO THE LONG SIDE. THE TWO-STORY FRONT PORCH HAS A SIMPLE GABLED ROOF FORMING A PEDIMENT. THE MAIN DOOR IS PANELED WITH FOUR SIDELIGHTS, AND SEVEN VERTICAL LIGHTS IN THE TRANSOME. MUCH OF THE GLASS IN THE HOUSE IS ORIGINAL. THE WINDOWS ARE NINE OVER NINE ON THE FIRST FLOOR AND NINE OVER SIX ON THE UPPER FLOOR. THE ORIGINAL HOUSE HAD TWO ROOMS ON EACH SIDE OF A CENTRAL HALL. THE GABLES HAVE FINE STONE CHIMNEYS WITH FIREPLACES ON BOTH FLOORS, EACH WITH ORIGINAL MANTELS. THE DEED RECORDS SUGGEST CONSTRUCTION BY J. L. FARQUHAR AND W. H. MCCUTCHON AROUND 1855 ON LAND PURCHASED FROM JOHN BANCROFT ROOT.

A 1912 PHOTOGRAPH SHOWS A LOG STRUCTURE TO THE SOUTHEAST OF THE HOUSE, PERHAPS THE ORIGINAL KITCHEN. A LATER ONE-STORY ADDITION TO THE REAR PROVIDED A CONNECTED KITCHEN. WHILE THE MAIN HOUSE IS RELATIVELY UNCHANGED, THE ADDITION UNDERWENT SIGNIFICANT MODIFICATION IN THE LATE TWENTIETH CENTURY.

DOCUMENTATION WAS UNDERTAKEN IN SUMMER 2003 BY GRADUATE STUDENTS SAMER AL-RATROUT, KATHLYN BLANCHARD AND LAURA BROWN, WITH ASSISTANCE FROM DR. RICHARD BURT AND DR. ULKER OREN. THE PROJECT WAS DIRECTED BY PROFESSOR DAVID G. WOODCOCK, FAIA, FOR THE HISTORIC RESOURCES IMAGING LABORATORY AT TEXAS A&M UNIVERSITY. THE PROJECT WAS SUPPORTED BY A GRANT FROM THE CURRENT OWNERS, PAT AND SHERRY ELLIOTT.

SAM HOUSTON, THE FIRST PRESIDENT OF THE REPUBLIC OF TEXAS, HAD A FARM AT CEDAR POINT, NEAR GALVESTON, AND HOMES IN HUNTSVILLE AND INDEPENDENCE. AFTER HIS DEATH IN 1863 HIS WIDOW, MARGARET LEA, REPORTEDLY MOVED TO THIS HOUSE WITH SEVEN OF HER EIGHT CHILDREN. A DEED OF PURCHASE FROM JAMES L. FARQUHAR IS DATED FEBRUARY 1866. MRS. HOUSTON DIED OF YELLOW FEVER IN DECEMBER 1867. HER DAUGHTER, MAGGIE, LIVED IN THE HOUSE UNTIL 1898, WHEN IT WAS SOLD TO THE WILLIAMS FAMILY, WHO REMAINED UNTIL 1983.

The population diminished when Independence refused to allow the railroad though their town. (*Library of Congress*)

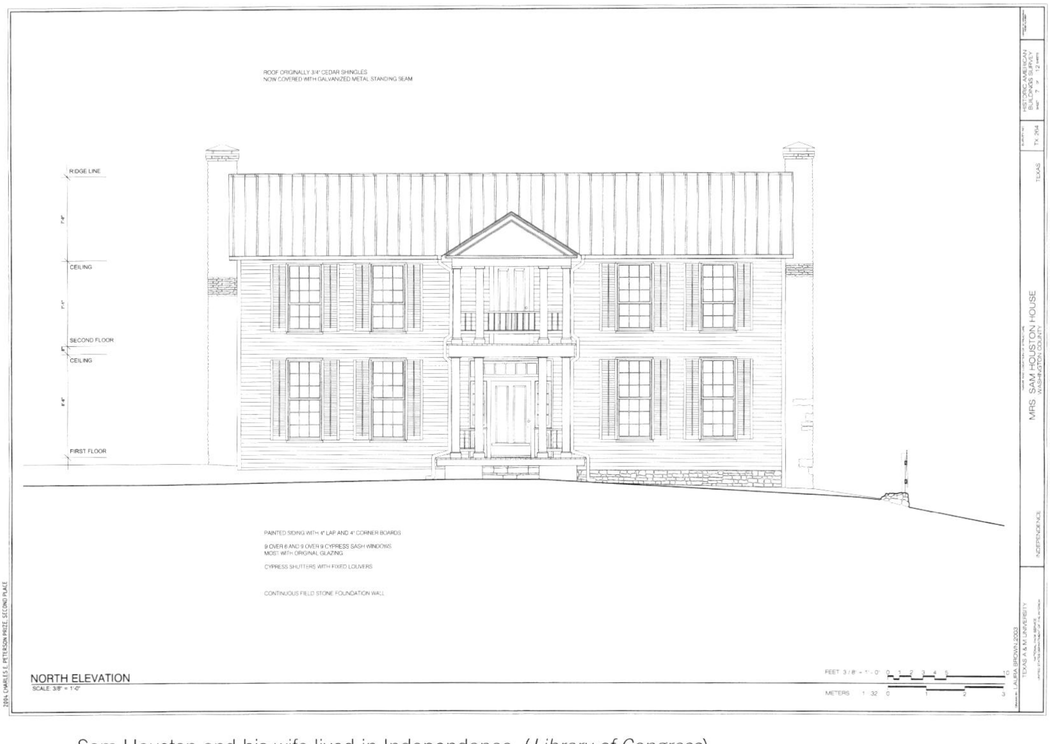

Sam Houston and his wife lived in Independence. (*Library of Congress*)

83

# Toyah, Texas

In 1879, W. T. Youngblood gathered his family and enough stock to supply a general store as he headed out of Midland, Texas, looking for a place to settle. He created a tent store in the area now known as Toyah, which was given its name by the indigenous tribes. Toyah translates to running water. The town eventually landed on the Texas and Pacific Railway in 1880, bringing stock and people to the city. Youngblood saved enough money to build a one-room adobe general store. The town of Toyah began to flourish.

A few houses popped up, and in 1881 when the first train arrived, Toyah came alive. Soon after, the post office arrived, and the Overland Stage Company began carrying passengers from Fort Davis to Fort Stockton. As the town developed into a shipping town for ranchers, restaurants, and saloons arrived. Youngblood continued adding to his general store with living quarters, a lobby, and a dining room. His general mercantile became a store and hotel combined.

Detective Charles Siringo arrived in Toyah in 1882 to investigate cattle rustling due to the copious ranches and cattle shipping from the area. Siringo was a bit of a celebrity cowboy in his time. By the end of his career, he had over twenty-two years of experience, captured hundreds of outlaws, and met several notorious bad guys. Toyah had a mix of good and evil like other wild west towns.

In 1885, Texas Ranger Captain James Gillespie established a camp in Toyah, and the area was about to utilize this law enforcement. In August 1885, Reeves County Sheriff John Morris had been drinking heavily and decided to board the train from Pecos to Toyah to find a man named Jep Clayton, a gunfighter and an all-around lousy guy known to get away with murder. When Sheriff Morris arrived in Toyah, he began placing demands on Captain Gillespie, which did not go over well with the captain. Sheriff Morris had a reputation for abusing alcohol excessively and using his authority to get his way. He said, "I run Pecos, and damned if I don't run Toyah."

The sheriff stomped away and went straight to the saloon, where he continued raising his intoxication level. As the evening continued, he began picking fights with other patrons and waving his gun. Captain Gillespie sent a group of Rangers to the saloon to contain and arrest the sheriff.

Four Rangers arrived at the saloon to find Sheriff Morris cursing up a storm and waving his pistol. They ordered him to stop, but he began firing on the Rangers instead. His first shot missed, but his second shot connected, hitting and instantly killing Private Thomas Nigh. A gunfight ensued. Sheriff Morris received five bullet wounds to the chest, and the saloon owner took shots to both legs. Private Nigh remained in Toyah as fellow Rangers buried his body in the local cemetery. Sheriff

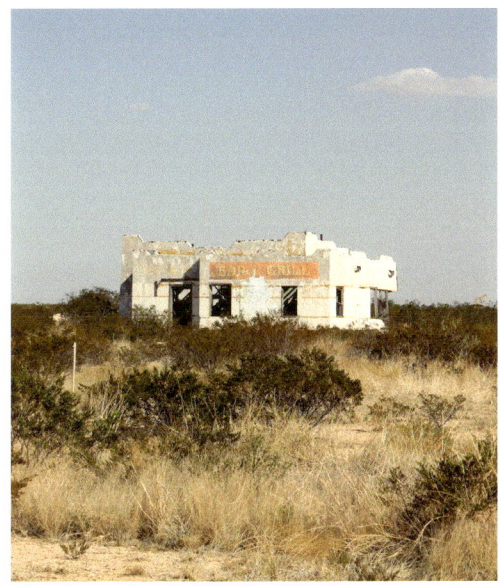
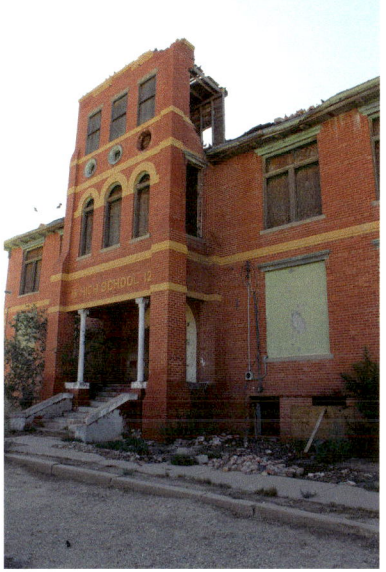

*Above left:* Much of Toyah was destroyed by a tornado in 2004. (*Nicholas Henderson*)

*Above right:* The community began as a trading post for large area ranches. (*Nicholas Henderson*)

Morris held on to life just long enough to be transported to a hotel where they could tend to his injuries. He died moments later, and his body went back to Pecos.

Toyah continued to grow under the watchful eyes of the Rangers, and in 1894 the community constructed its first school. It started with one room and teacher but grew as the town thrived.

Despite the protection of the Rangers, Toyah remained a wild west town filled with outlaws ready to cause trouble. In September 1896, the saloon experienced another violent attack while a former Ranger and Reeves County Sheriff visited his family. Better known as Bud, George Frazer was in a bloody feud with Killin' James Miller, who served as Pecos City marshal. Miller was perhaps one of the most violent men in the wild west. Despite being an officer of the law, he was also an outlaw and professional hitman. He didn't drink, smoke, or use distasteful language. He dressed sharply and fooled many people with his angelic personality and appearance. He even attended church regularly.

The duo met in 1891 when Frazer served as the Reeves County Sheriff and sought a deputy. During the interview process, Frazer kept his questions to a minimum. After all, grilling with questions wasn't proper cowboy etiquette. A few years later, Frazer would realize this was a grave mistake.

About the time Miller became sheriff, horse theft and robbery increased. Deputy Miller patrolled the area but never seemed to capture any outlaws. Eventually,

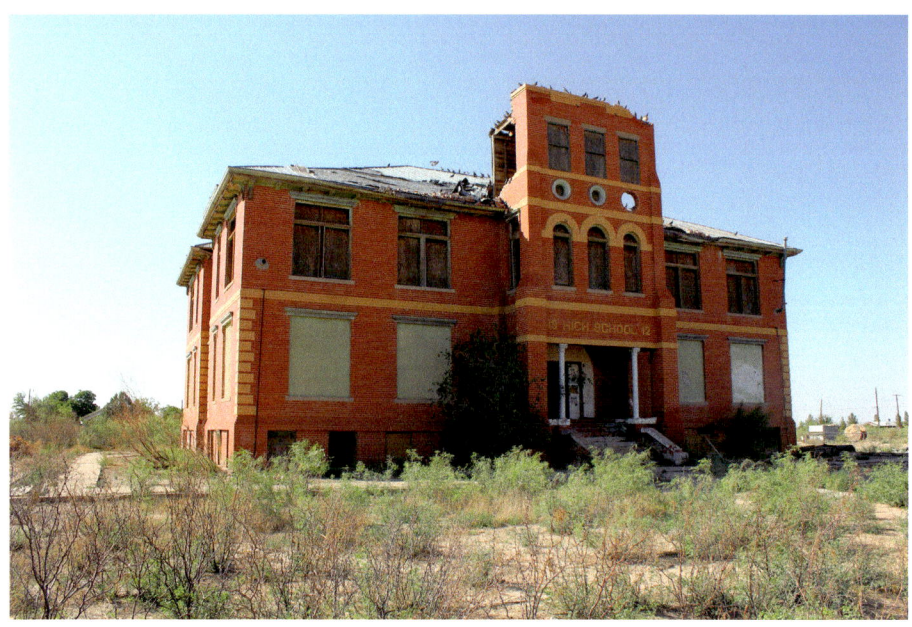

The first train arrived in Toyah in 1881. (*Nicholas Henderson*)

Frazer began to suspect Miller as the culprit and confronted him. However, Miller denied the charges, and Frazer lacked the evidence to fire or charge his deputy with criminal activity. Time passed, and Miller showed his true colors when he killed a Mexican prisoner who knew too much about Miller's unlawful actions. Frazer fired Miller, and their feud commenced. The two parted ways.

The men met as opposing candidates for the 1892 Pecos sheriff election a year later. Despite Frazer's win, Miller managed to get elected Pecos City marshal. Miller then surrounded himself with professional gunslingers to work as his deputies.

In May of the following year, Frazer left town on business. Miller hatched a plan to stage a shootout in which a bullet would fatally strike Frazer. However, his plan dissolved when a witness overheard it and promptly contacted Frazer. Miller and two other men found themselves fighting conspiracy charges to kill Frazer. Miller had already released one of his men to silence the witness who contacted Frazer. With no surviving witness, the courts did not have a case, and the three men were set free. Miller lost his job but walked away free until he met his rival on the streets of Pecos.

On April 18, 1894, Frazer came across Miller in the street and yelled a warning before firing his first shot to strike Miller's arm. Miller fired back but missed. Frazer proceeded to unload his weapon firing direct hits to Miller's chest. Frazer walked away, thinking he had finally ended the feud. However, Miller's men dragged his

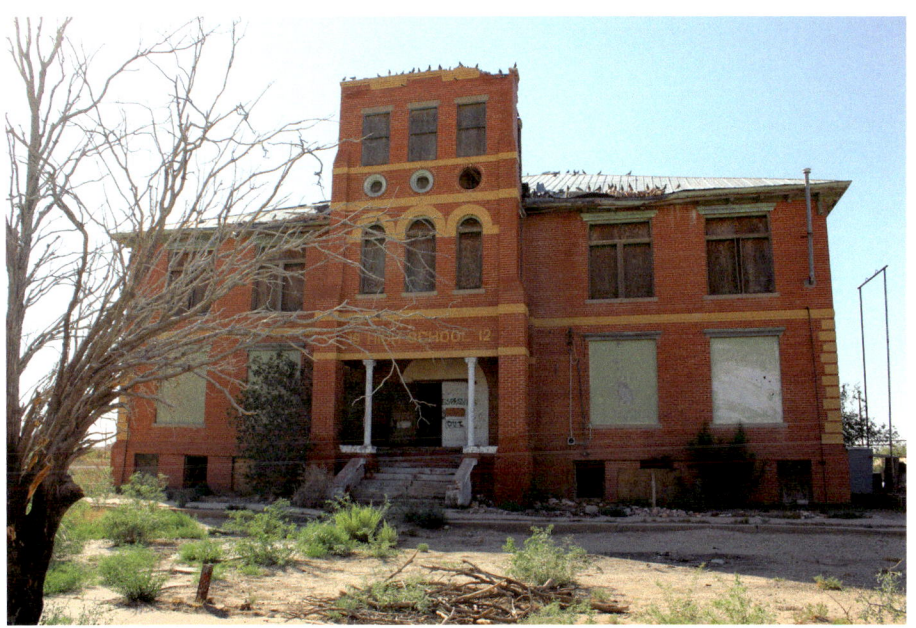

Toyah became a major cattle-shipping stop along the tracks. (*Nicholas Henderson*)

body to safety and, upon examination, found Miller wore a heavy metal plate under his heavy jacket. He would require time to mend but be far from dying.

After losing the next sheriff election, Frazer moved to New Mexico. When Frazer returned to Toyah to settle his affairs, he met up with Miller again. He shot him in the chest twice this time, and Miller barely flinched. Frazer was left frustrated and confused until he later pieced together the idea of Miller using a breastplate. The feud continued as a new attorney attempted to re-charge Miller with attempted murder.

Miller grew impatient and decided to go after another rival to relieve tension. His other feud was with a man named Barney Riggs, who was the brother-in-law of Bud Frazer. For unknown reasons, Riggs was the only man Miller ever feared, and with him dead, it was certain Frazer would come after Miller and provide an opportunity to rid the world of both enemies. In 1896, Miller sent two assassins to eliminate Riggs. Miller's fear of Riggs proved worthy. The would-be assassins barely nicked Riggs with a bullet before a gun fired at them. Riggs killed both of his attackers. He turned himself in, but after a trial, officials acquitted him.

Back to that fateful morning in September 1896, Frazer played a game of cards with some friends at the saloon. Miller stormed through the front door and shot Frazer directly in the face. Reports state that his head nearly left his body. Distraught over what just occurred, Frazer's sister turned a gun on Miller, who laughed as he threatened her with the same treatment as her brother. Miller faced a trial but was acquitted.

At least one man hung from the gallows in Toyah. On October 25, 1906, an African American named "Slab" Pitts moved to Toyah with his wife, Eva. Toyah prohibited African Americans from living within the city limits in the early formation. As Pitts rolled into town, the onlookers noted his wife was white and quickly set a plan into motion. A mob pulled Pitts from his bed, placing a noose around his neck. They drugged him through town and hung him from a telephone poll. Toyah attracted tragedy and death.

At its peak, the Toyah population reached just over 1,000 residents. The town held four stores, four churches, two hotels, two lumber yards, a drugstore, and two banks. Shallow oil fields had the town population for many years, but the Great Depression came in the 1930s and devastated Toyah. The town lost its shipping business as the companies re-routed. The population continued to spiral downward, and floods destroyed many buildings. Today, the population is around 100, and most buildings sit abandoned.

## Marfa, Texas

Marfa, Texas, is often considered a ghost town as it is desolate and, for the most part, uninhabited. The town has an operating courthouse, a few businesses, and even a town square, but seldom are any of the 1,700 people out and about. Despite being out in the desert, many people travel to Marfa as a tourist.

Established in 1883, Maria became a water stop and freight headquarters for Galveston, Harrisburg, and San Antonio Railway. A water stop allowed the steam

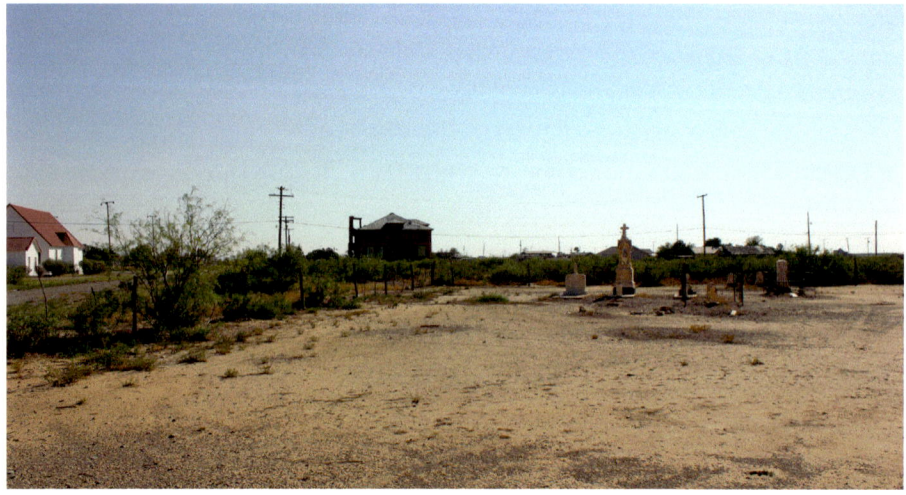

By 2000, the population had dropped to under 100 residents. (*Nicholas Henderson*)

engines to refill. The city's name came from a book one of the railroad executive's wives read at the time, Fyodor Dostoyevsky's *The Brothers Karamazov*.

Early in the history of Marfa, traveling salesmen and visitors came via trains. In 1885, Presidio County grew from Fort Davis to Marfa as the town grew. The three-story Renaissance revival-style courthouse adorned the city. The following year, Marfa had its first newspaper. By 1920, there were over 3,500 residents, a telephone service, a bank, and even fraternal organizations.

During the Mexican Revolution, the United States government sent troops to Marfa. They continued to increase the population with military and new residents. In the 1940s, the government constructed a prison of war camp nearby and, soon after, an army airfield. By 1945, the military helped increase the town's population to over 5,000. The following year, the military closed down both installations, ending their economic and cultural influence on the city.

Due to Marfa's proximity to Mexico, the United States government placed mounted watchmen to patrol the area in 1924 to deter illegal immigrants smuggling liquor during prohibition. Long after the ban, the need for security against drugs continued in this area, and in 1989, the government built an aerostat station to help control drug smuggling across the border.

One strange sight in Marfa is the luxury boutique in the desert. In 2005, two artists, Michael Elmgreen and Ingar Dragset, erected a sculpture that resembles a Prada store. The small store featured the Prada logo on two big black signs and awnings. The artist wanted to make a statement about high-priced commercialism. Miuccia Prada could have displayed anger toward the critique of her company but instead donated shoes and purses from her 2005 collection to complete the store.

The artists stated, "This architectural entity of a luxury boutique had suddenly become present in our culture, and we are all starting to get used to it."

Almost instantly, visitors destroyed the art with graffiti, and the purses and shoes disappeared. The duo stepped to clean up their sculpture, and today Marfa has unique road signs directing people to the "store." The original idea was to build a structure that would dissolve in time, and Mother Nature reclaimed the area. However, it remains tall and proud in the desert landscape years later.

Are fake Prada stores not scary? How about strange unidentified lights in the sky? While scientific research indicates these lights are most likely atmospheric reflections. Most notably, the reflection of automobile lights passing by and reflecting off the surrounding nature. However, witnesses to the light display feel they might be paranormal in nature or visitors from another planet. This display is so popular that Marfa has identified a Marfa Lights Viewing Center.

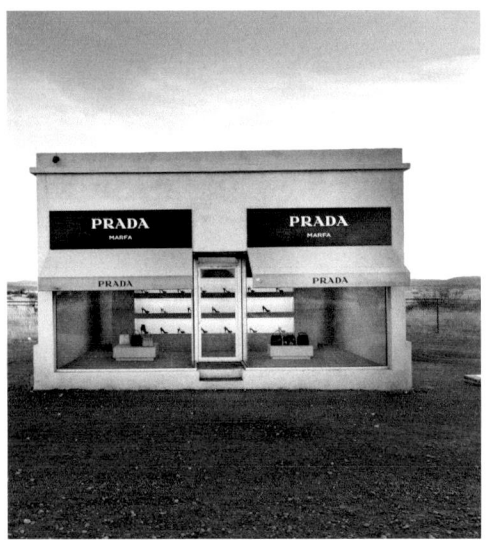 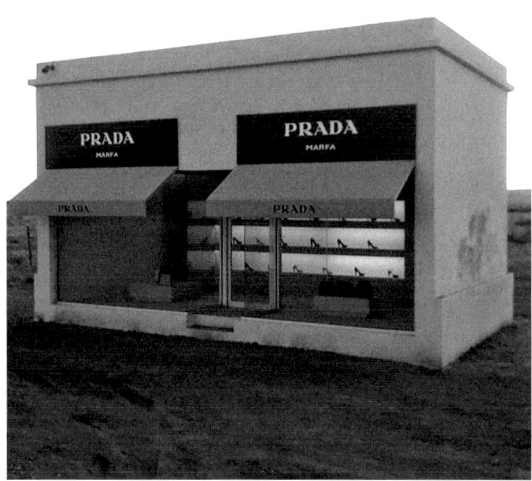

*Above left:* In the early 1880s, Marfa was a water stop. (*Carol Highsmith*)

*Above right:* Marfa is known for the strange lights that appear at night. The first recorded sighting was in 1883. (*Carol Highsmith*)

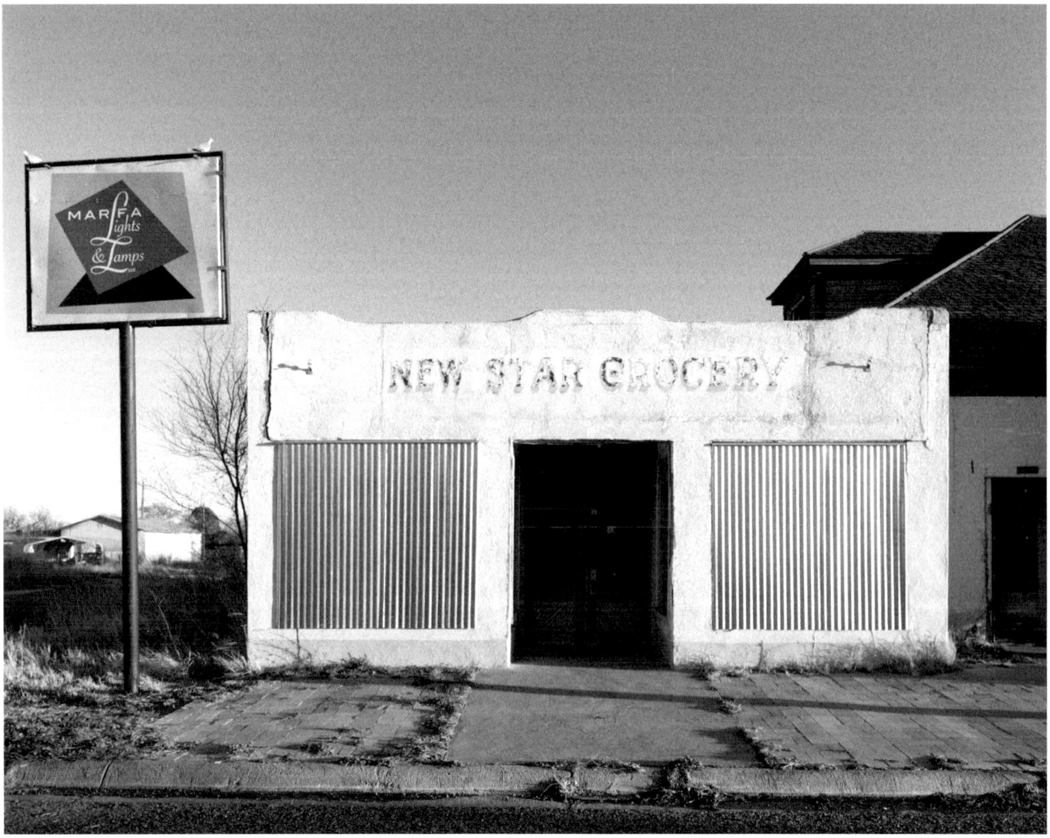

Marfa is the only known ghost town with a replica of a Prada store. (*Carol Highsmith*)

The Marfa lights were first noted in 1883 by a cowhand driving cattle. He believed the lights came from the campfire of an Apache tribe in the area. Others reported lights over the years; they did not find ashes or campfires after investigating. These were the times long before automobiles and outside light sources.

UFO (unidentified flying object) enthusiasts hold out hope of the lights belonging to travelers from other planets contacting Earth. Dozens of witnesses' report seeing the same phenomenon. While these lights differ from the average UFO sighting, they still fascinate young and old spectators.

The lights appear differently depending on the viewer's location. Some viewers will see mysterious orbs of light that suddenly appear. The spheres can pulsate or remain stationary. They can also jet across the sky and dance in a way that no average vehicle or aircraft can move. Witnesses state they hover, twinkle, merge, split in two, flicker, float up, and dart away. They appear red, white, orange, yellow, green, or blue.

Now that Marfa is virtually a ghost town, the strange lights add mystery and an ominous feel to the tiny village.

## Catarina

Located in Dewitt County, Catarina, Texas, was once a thriving city with over 50,000 residents. Locals consider the founding and success of the town to fall on multiple people as it varied over the years.

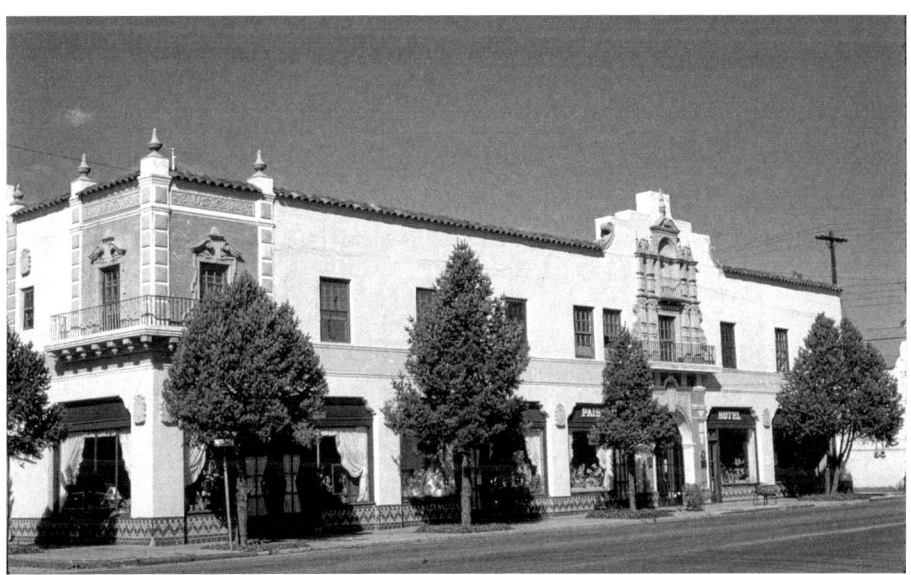

Marfa served as an airfield during World War Two. (*Carol Highsmith*)

At the start, Catarina was nothing more than a large ranch owned by Coleman-Fulton Pasture Company. Asher Richardson founded the city of Asherton and wanted to build a railroad connecting the town to Artesia Wells. He agreed to let the ranch establish a railroad depot on their land. The railroad allowed Catarina to transport cattle and cattle equipment.

Joseph Green managed Catarina Ranch. Green worked with Asherton to make the depot the ranch headquarters and establish a small community surrounding the depot. By 1910, the area had a post office, bunk house, a hotel, a commissary, and a small school. Walter Mitson worked as the town's bookkeeper, depot agent, postmaster, and justice of the peace.

In 1915, Catarina gained roads, sidewalks, and flowing water. Investors Clint Kearney, J. E. Jarret, and H. V. Wheeler worked together to construct a town plan with broad streets, running water, electricity, telephone lines, and a fire department. The agriculture flourished with the ranch, bringing in fruit trees for lush orchards. The town's popularity increased when Charles Taft, brother to President of the United States William Taft, built a mansion in Catarina.

By 1925, the small town had grown to more than 2,000 residents. Officials built a new, two-story hotel with power and a working telephone, the majestic Royal Palms hotel. The bright, red brick exterior allowed grand palm trees to stand in glory surrounding the hotel.

When the water dried up and the Great Depression hit, Catarina suffered and never fully recovered. The hotel remained open until sometime in the 1950s before facing abandonment. By 1990, there were only forty-five residents in the town.

Charles Lad from Kansas developed the town and named it after his wife, Catherine. However, the Catarina Ranch existed long before Lad and held over 225,000 acres of land. Legend tells the Catarina Ranch received its name from a Mexican woman who served as a cook on the ranch and died via a Comanche attack. The original headquarters burned to the ground, and a new structure replaced the old. It lay on top of the old, charred form. The stream near this location received the name Catarina Creek. The lore caused local children to deem the place a "ghost house." Yet another tale is the ranch name honored Santa Catarina de Siena or the paeon saint of everything from fire prevention to temptation.

In 1999, a guest at the Royal Palms reported he was watching television when he looked away from the screen and glanced into the hallway to see a dark grey mist float by his room.

In 2020, Catarina lost the majority on one of its longest-standing buildings, the Royal Palms Hotel. Ownership of the hotel exchanged hands many times. In 2013, Fiona Fan, one of the eight members of the Peony River investors, stated that her

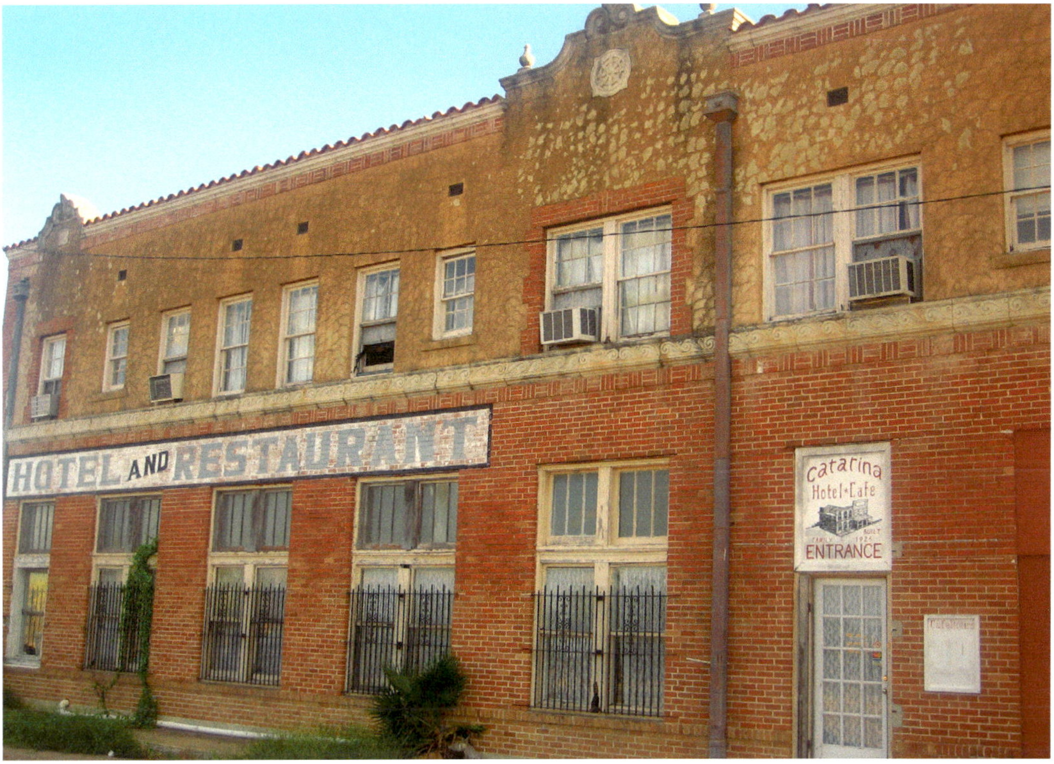

The town may have been named for the wife of a railroad executive. (*John Margolis*)

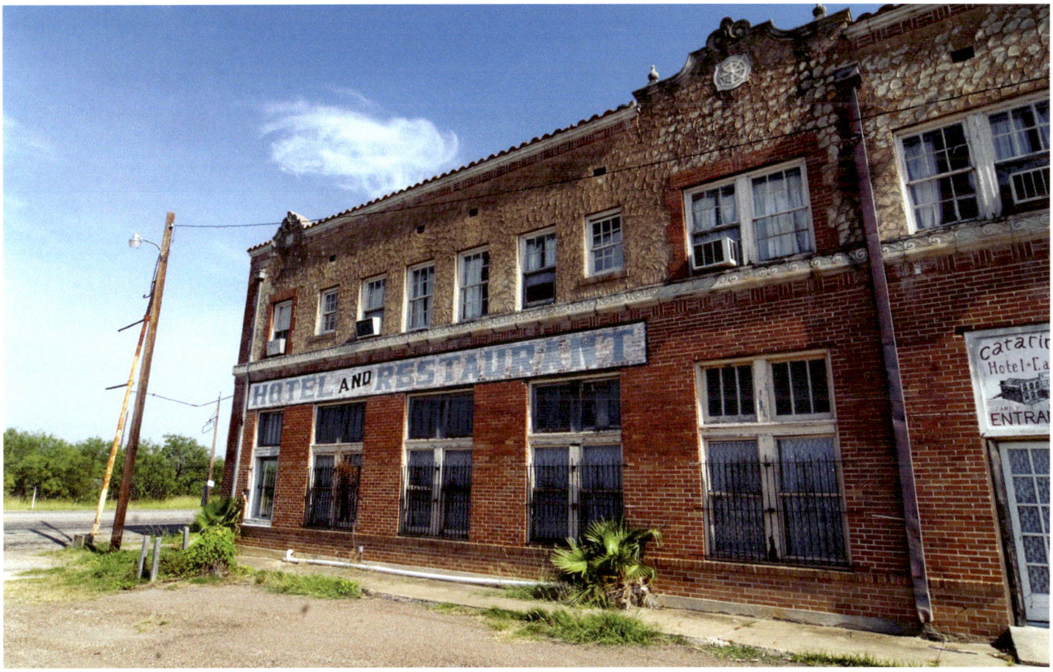

Water needed to be pumped into the area to keep the crops alive. Without water, there would be no farming. (*Richard Flores*)

aunt drove past the hotel and immediately felt the structure needed restoration as a piece of history. The nearby oil fields still boomed, and the investment was wise. The Peony River investors planned to restore the hotel. The renovation took about two years to complete and included code and modern conveniences, but it remained faithful to the historical heritage of the original building. They re-opened the restaurant and hotel in 2015 as Palm Suite and Inn but closed a few years later as the oil boom mowed.

Human life abandoned the Royal Palms a second time. The final demise came from a typical Texas thunderstorm. Several fire departments responded, but it was too late. Due to the hotel's age, the investment company could not insure the property. All that remains today are the hotel's exterior walls and the frayed palm trees lining the front entrance. The Peony River investors are hopeful of restoring the hotel once more.

# Helena

What is better than a ghost town? How about a ghost town filled with ghosts? Helena, Texas, is located approximately 70 miles southeast of San Antonio. The area grew in population as a road traveling through the area transported goods to and from Mexico.

In 1852, Thomas Ruckman and Dr. Lewis Owings founded Helena at the site of a Mexican trading post called Alamita. The men renamed the area Helana to honor Dr. Owing's wife, Helen. They envisioned their business partnership would lead to a metropolitan area due to the popularity of the roadway. Ruckman opened a general store and built a small gristmill to grind grains for flour. He also took the role of the town's first postmaster. The city continued to grow, and the duo promoted Helena as a contender for the Karnes County official seat. Helena held the county seat from 1854 until 1894.

The high traffic flow of Mexican import and gold bullion enabled Dr. Owings to operate a line with four-horse coaches from San Antonio and Victoria. Regarding carts, the main incidents of the Cart War occurred around Helena. The so-called war erupted in 1857 and would hold national and international repercussions. Historians agree that the underlying cause of the fight stemmed from ethnic and racial hostilities between Texans and Mexican Texas. Utilizing ox carts allowed Mexican carters to transport items fast, which angered their competitors. Mexican carters fell victim to violence, and authorities did little to nothing to stop the attacks. After a solid month of bloodshed, the violence stopped.

During its prime, Helena boasted a courthouse, jail, church, Masonic lodge, drugstore, hotels, blacksmith shop, saloons, and general stores. A school and newspaper followed. Employment opportunities arose, but some jobs were hard to fill. For example, the longest term for a sheriff in Helena was six months, and the shortest was six days. Helena gained the reputation as "the toughest town on earth" and the birthplace of the Helena Duel, which tied two combattants at the wrist with a strong rope. Each fighter received a knife with a three-inch blade and instructions to slash one another. The match ended when one of the competitors bled out and died.

In 1884, Helena's fate took a turn for the worse. Wealthy ranch owner William Butler's son died during a shootout. When no one came forward to admit their sin, Butler punished the entire city and vowed: "to kill the town that killed his son." He contacted the head of the railroad and gave the right of way to construct the rails through his ranch, which would bypass the town of Helena. By 1886, the city began its descent. In 1894, Helena lost the county seat, and the population diminished until Helena became a ghost town.

Paranormal researchers believe Helena has many hot spots, but Ruckman's former home and the old courthouse are two of the most popular. Paranormal investigations found evidence of electric voice phenomenon (EVP), shadow people,

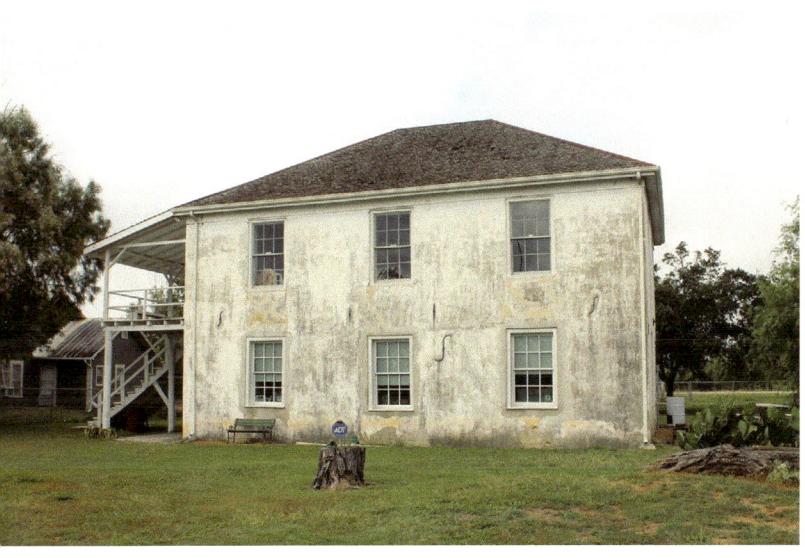
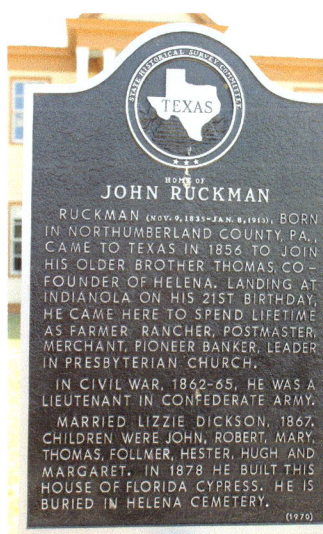

*Above left:* When a local rancher blamed the town for his son's death, he vowed to destroy Helena. (*Renelibrary*)

*Above right:* Known for the Helena Duel, this town was tough. (*Darryl Pearson*)

moving objects, and even physical attacks. Some claim to feel a demonic or evil presence in the Ruckman mansion and believe this could be related to its violent history of Helena.

The Russell Rush Haunted Tour's evidence included sound recordings that appeared to say "mommy" and "Christopher."

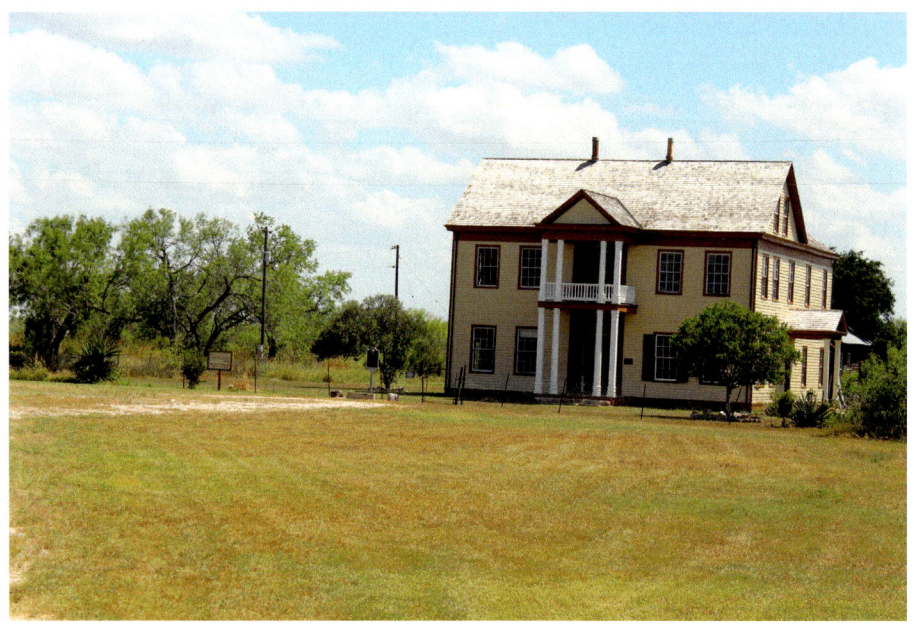

Thomas Ruckman was one of the two founders of Helena. (*Darryl Pearson*)